Eloise

Love & Prayers.

May Borsheim

God's Little Girls

May Borsheim

WESTBOW
PRESS®
A DIVISION OF THOMAS NELSON
& ZONDERVAN

WestBow Press books may be ordered through booksellers or by contacting:

WestBow Press
A Division of Thomas Nelson & Zondervan
1663 Liberty Drive
Bloomington, IN 47403
www.westbowpress.com
1 (866) 928-1240

ISBN: 978-1-9736-1811-9 (sc)
ISBN: 978-1-9736-1812-6 (hc)
ISBN: 978-1-9736-1810-2 (e)

Library of Congress Control Number: 2018901373

Print information available on the last page.

WestBow Press rev. date: 03/19/2018

CONTENTS

Dedication

Dedicated to those who have been physically and sexually abused. You are not alone, and there is hope.

And - to all those who helped in the creation of this book. Without you, none of this would be possible.

ᴼFOREWORD

Memories of one's childhood experiences are mostly vague or limited, triggered only by specific sights, sounds, or smells that may or may not make sense. Of those we do recall, some memories are joyous – while others are painful and bitter. Combined, these memories, our experiences – good and bad – form the individual we are today. While no one "wants" to experience neglect or abuse, those who have recognize that those collective experiences shaped the individual (character, personality, passions, etc.) they are today. You may have bias or prejudice, hate and anger locked up inside...or you may have chosen to lean on God and others for support and let it go. Life is a journey – and this journey is worth sharing in hopes that others will find peace in light of bittersweet memories.

INTRODUCTION

In the 1930s and 40s, child abuse (or spousal abuse) was not openly discussed. It was gossip on the tongues of co-workers, neighbors, and acquaintances unable to help – in any fashion. Some people do the best they can – but in many cases, it is not enough. But God – yes God can and does so exceedingly and abundantly above all we can ask for, and in ways we never imagined.

This is my story - about the lives of my sister and me – from birth to early adulthood. It is entirely true, though names and some locations are changed to shelter those still living.

CHAPTER 1
The Early Years

My mother's name was Velma, and my father's name was Eldon. Momma, as we called her, came from a large family. She was one of 10 children and the oldest daughter; five girls (Velma, Jenny, Tess, Lottie, and Betsy) and five boys (Gary, Greg, Johnny, Emmitt, and Ben). Large families were common and almost a necessity in a farming community. Daddy had two brothers (Billy and Charles) and two sisters (Lucile and Jane). I am not sure where he was in the birth order, and we did not do much with them as a family. His family moved around frequently for work.

Daddy was slightly older than Momma was and was somewhat of a sweet talker if you know what I mean. There is little I know of their early-married life, only bits and pieces of information have been tossed out in conversations over time. It was said they met at a dance in town and fell in love right away. They married after a brief courtship.

Details of my early childhood years may have been completely lost if I had not found our baby books, what a blessing that was. As I read through them, the memories came pouring back. It was the beginning of a journey for me, a trip back in time through memories long forgotten.

My sister and I were born in Douglas, Wyoming. Mom and Dad married in early 1937, and shortly after that, they moved to Wyoming to find work. My sister (Mary Jane, I called her Sissy when we were little) is almost nine months older than I am. She was one and a half pounds at birth and was born in the sixth month of Momma's pregnancy in October of 1937. She was in the hospital for quite some time before Mom and Dad could bring her home. It is a miracle such a tiny baby survived in those days. Within a month Momma became pregnant again, with me. She was in her seventh month of pregnancy when she went into labor, and this time she did not make it to the hospital - I (May Janette) was born at home in July of 1938. They placed me on an open oven door in a shoebox to keep warm. After a three-week stay in the hospital, I came home - weighing three pounds two ounces, and I was ten inches long. Mom and Dad could not afford much – let alone large hospital bills. I am sure they did not have insurance at the time.

It must have been overwhelming for my mother – having to care for two, very tiny babies. Mom was 19 when my sister was born and 20 with me. I am sure we kept her busy washing diapers (no disposable ones back then) and feeding us on a schedule. She likely got little sleep caring for two tiny, premature girls. I often wonder how she dealt with the stress. It is a miracle from God that both of us survived such a rough start. My Grandmother told us stories of how Momma would place a teacup over our heads and her wedding ring over our hands and how she used just one baby buggy for both of us

Momma kept a record of my weight for the first eighteen months of my life, starting at three pounds and two ounces at birth.

- Two and a half pounds at three weeks (apparently I lost some weight), three pounds at one month, eight pounds at six months, twelve pounds at one year and sixteen pounds at eighteen months.

Mom had written in my sister's baby book as she was weaning her from the bottle that she would fill my sister's bottle with water and mine with milk and Sissy would switch bottles with me. I thought that was so funny. I think of all the hours of care she must have put into our first two years of our lives. *"I will praise you for I am wonderfully made. Marvelous are your works; and that my soul knows very well"*, Psalms 139:14 (NKJV).

Our little family lived in Douglas WY for a very short time, just over a year. Long enough for Sissy and I to be born. Work was not plentiful there, so Mom and Dad moved back to Missouri with Mom's parents for a short while before finally settling in Waterloo IA. Dad landed a good job with a local meat packing company that paid well and had good benefits – something our family needed. Sissy was nearly three, and I was two, and this was the beginning of our journey.

Clearly, I was too young to remember us living in Wyoming or Missouri, so my earliest memories are of us living in Waterloo IA. It is hard to remember everything, but family stories are enough to help me make recreate events and make some sense of things.

My dad was a thin man, a little taller than medium height from what I recall. He was a heavy smoker. My mother was tall, slender and always spoke with a gentle, yet confident voice. At some point, after we moved to Waterloo, things changed for Daddy. He began to drink and lose control of his emotions – and began hitting us. I am sure this change in him did not happen overnight, it is the way I recall it though.

All of us were afraid of him coming home angry if he had a bad day at work. We would be extra quiet and try hard to be good. As little girls, we learned not to make Daddy mad because we all would pay for it with a beating. One of my earliest memories was at the age of four. We were getting ready to go somewhere, and I would not put my shoes on. To get us to mind without a fuss, Dad told us the "boogieman" would get us if we did not listen. In spite of this, I was determined not to put my shoes on, so I hid on the basement steps to avoid punishment. All of a sudden, the light in the basement went out, and I heard a gruff, garbled voice coming from somewhere nearby. Terrified, I went screaming back up the stairs, thinking it was the boogieman - then I fainted on the floor just outside the door. I never forgot that – as a four-year-old it frightened me tremendously and affected me for years, leaving me with a fear of the dark. I learned much later from my aunt Betsy that Dad was trying to scare me. He put on an overcoat and a mask, went through the outside basement door, and turned out the light. I think at the time he was trying to scare me into submission, and it backfired.

When Sissy and I were young, we always got hard spankings. We would comfort one another, cuddling together as we fell asleep. We tried to be good little girls, and we were always looking out for each other. There was a time when I was playing in the living room by myself, and there was a tube of ointment and a large needle lying on the table beside Daddy's chair. Curious – and just being a kid - I picked up the needle and started poking the tube of ointment (I do not know whatever gave me the idea to do that). When I finished poking holes in the ointment tube, I went on to play elsewhere and forgot all about it. Later, as I was playing with my dolls, I heard Sissy screaming and crying. I ran to the living room with fear racing through my body - Daddy was beating Sissy with the heel of his shoe because the tube of ointment was full of holes. Sissy was crying loudly and repeatedly saying "I didn't do it, Daddy," and my heart broke for her. I felt horrified – I cried out and confessed, "Daddy she didn't do it - I did." I was ready to take my punishment, but he did not stop. I cried a long time; my heart broke for her, but I could not stop him or change what took place. My heart still hurts when I think of it. Sissy and I would always hug each other after these episodes, but not this time. It was just the beginning of the beatings for us, and I know Momma took her share of them too. When Daddy would come home angry, we were sent to our room. Crying and shaking with fear for Momma, Sissy and I would cling to each other praying for Daddy not to be so angry and mean. Momma would have black and blue marks on her arms and sometimes on her face, which she tried to cover up with makeup. She was good at covering up the bruises and emotionally pushing aside the hurt and fear. Daddy would get mean and angry over nothing; we never knew when he would "blow up." He also did not believe in God, and he hated for us to even say grace before our meals. On one occasion, Sissy and I started to say a quick prayer before our evening meal, and Daddy picked up a pitcher full of water and hurled it at us. That evening, we did not eat our meal at the table. We went to our room crying, listening to the verbal and physical beating Momma was getting. He was home a lot; it seemed like one or two days a week. He often appeared sickly, and on few times we noticed he would cough up blood.

As if it were not enough living with an abusive father, several kids in our neighborhood would pick on me. Sissy, however, would stop them in their tracks. I recall one time we were playing with our new little red wagon on the sidewalk in front of our house, and the neighbor boys came and took it from us. Instead of crying and getting upset Sissy went after the two boys pushed them down, bringing our red wagon home triumphantly! She was the bold one - I was the timid one. Momma always kept an eye us as we played and she taught us that it was ok to stand our ground. I am sure she would have stepped in and helped if it were necessary but Sissy took care of things promptly and fairly

The three of us were close – Sissy, Momma and I would have good times when Daddy was not around. My mother was a hard-working woman who kept her home well. She would teach us games she played as a child. Coming from a large family, they did not have many toys growing up, so they learned to make toys from standard household items. Momma would save soup cans for us to play with. She would open the cans upside down, and we would use them in our play grocery store. Momma would come and shop at "our store" that she set up in our basement. We also used empty packages of every kind (egg cartons, cake mix boxes, etc.) - we were well supplied! It was our rainy day get away. Not only did we have fun, I felt we were learning at the same time. We learned many outdoor games as well. Sissy and I loved it when Momma did things with us.

As little girls, our lives resembled a roller coaster ride – many ups and downs, twists and turns. Work was not always steady for Daddy, so we moved where work was available at the time. We had happy times alongside the scary, unsure times and learned to adapt to change at an early age. When Sissy and I were about five and six, the family moved to a farm in Missouri. Mom and Dad took over the farm from one of Mom's brothers, and it included all the livestock and some equipment. It was summer time when we moved in, and we just knew this was going to be an adventure for all of us. I do not recall why we took over the farm, likely because of layoffs at the packing plant where Daddy worked, but it was a good move – good for all of us. To our surprise, Daddy did not drink. Actually, for the first time in a long time, we saw Daddy not drinking or angry. Living on the farm was great, we had good times. I can still remember how that old barn seemed so big to us. This farm was truly in the middle of nowhere. We were city girls; we knew nothing about country living, and suddenly we were thrust into a new way of life – the "country girl" life. Right away, we were tasked with small chores like gathering eggs and filling the water tanks for the livestock; Sissy and I each taking a turn at the pump handle to bring the water up (this was not turning on a faucet). There was a momma cat in the barn along with her three pure white kittens with blue eyes. We named them Snow White, Snowflake and Snowball. At milking time, they would wait for their milk, all three sitting atop the bottom half of the double barn door.

Daddy plowed a large patch of ground up for Momma's garden behind the house. It was a beautiful garden. We helped Momma weed it, and she would cook the fresh vegetables from the garden. Momma was a great cook, and she made everything from scratch. Sissy and I would watch her bake using the fresh eggs we would gather every day.

Sissy and I loved playing outside on the farm! One sunny afternoon we were outside playing with some old pie tins Momma gave us. We were making pies and cakes out of mud – being good little "homemakers" when one of us got the idea that eggs were a necessary ingredient in our pies to taste as good as Mommas. Off to the henhouse, we went for some eggs, which we proudly added to our muddy mixtures. Of course, Momma was watching us use her fresh eggs to create our "organic" pies, and she promptly put an end to it. She took our pies and dumped them over the back fence - all the while instructing us that real eggs were for her baking and not for our playtime concoctions. We were sent to our room for the rest of the afternoon. I do not think she ever let Daddy know about it.

Farm living for us included various chores but there were times we could make work a little fun - and burning brush piles was one of them. The whole family would go down to the field at the bottom of the hill behind the garden to burn the brush pile that Daddy created by clearing out the bottomland. Momma would bring hotdogs, buns, and marshmallows and we would sit together and eat our fill watching the sparks fluttering up to the sky. These were good days – but regretfully they did not last long. Daddy got a job back at the meat packing company and in the blink of an eye (at least to a young girl) the farm and livestock were sold. Mom and Dad purchased a big two-story house back in Waterloo, Iowa.

When school let out for the summer, Sissy and I went to our Grandparents for two weeks while Momma and Daddy went to Waterloo to make moving arrangements. Sissy and I had a hard time leaving the farm, and we hated to leave all our pets behind. Momma did promise we could take our dog Sonny along, which helped to ease our sadness. We did not have many toys to take but we packed our favorite ones, and the rest were placed in the estate sale. As Sissy and I watched the auctioneer preparing to sell our things, things that meant so much to us, we tried to imagine what our new place was going to be like. Would we find new friends at our new school? Would Daddy start drinking again? When the horses came up for sale Momma, Sissy and I cried. We loved those horses, we called them Tom and Jerry, and they had been a vital part of our daily life. I cannot remember which one we used to ride to school but he would take us and drop us off then he would go back home. When it was time for school to let out in the afternoon, he would be there waiting for us. We only got this privilege during bad weather otherwise; we walked to school, which was about two miles up and down (yes, both ways) hilly dirt roads. We did not mind walking a bit - I can still see in my mind's eye that long road to school, the crisp morning air of those first fall days. Our dog Sunny would always follow us for the first couple of days, and we would have to scold him and send him back home. It was as if he was trying to tell us, "Who is going to play with me now?" He was a great dog. Living on a farm in those days meant you had to make due and often take care of certain problems yourself. At times, that meant veterinary work. When Sonny's tail became matted with cockleburs, they began to embed into the fleshy part of the tail causing big sores, so Daddy had to chop the bad part of his tail off. I know he felt better, but he mournfully carried his tail around for three days...then buried it! I can also credit Sonny for saving lives. Sissy and I were playing out near the garden with him one day when he started growling, standing and pointing like a bird dog. Momma and Daddy had been working nearby. All of a sudden, Sonny lunged forward and came up with a big snake, shaking it violently and snapping its head off. Daddy said it was a blue racer snake, very poisonous. Once again, God had His protective hand upon us. *"No evil shall befall you, nor any plague come near your dwelling. For He shall give His angels charge over you to keep you in all your ways"*, Psalms 91:10 – 11 (NKJV).

This would be the last time we would know what it was like not to have a daddy so angry all the time.

CHAPTER 2
Country Roads Left Behind

As I look back at our days of farm living it is hard to imagine how things might have been if we stayed there. I think of how wonderful it may have been to remain there as a family where, for a brief stitch in time, life was good. Circumstances and events in our life can cause us to travel into deep valleys and dark pathways. To begin with, the move back to Iowa was not stress-free – halfway through the move to our new home things began to fall apart - literally when the moving trailer we were pulling, started to sway and bounce out of control and almost flipped our car. Daddy, spouting foul words, managed to regain control and get the car and trailer safely to the side of the road – it was a scary for all of us. Not having the luxury of a cell phone, it was up to Daddy to find help, and from where we stopped he had to walk quite a distance. He came back a few hours later after finding help through the kindness strangers who let him use their home phone (my how times have changed!). It was another two hours before our family in Waterloo were able to pick us up. Just us, we had to leave the car and trailer. It was such a relief to see my Aunt and Uncle coming to our aid. It felt like we sat in that car for days waiting for help to arrive. It was in the early morning hours before we got to Waterloo - we were exhausted. Sissy and I spent the next week with Aunt Tess while Momma got the house ready and Daddy and Uncle Byron went to pick up our belongings and the trailer we left behind. When move-in day finally arrived, Momma picked us up to take us to our new home. We were bubbling over with excitement, having to wait that week seemed like waiting forever for two little girls. It was the beginning of summer, and we looked forward to making new friends. Our room was wonderful - big enough for us to house all our toys. Our school was only six blocks away. In the fall I was starting the second grade, Sissy the third. The first few weeks were busy helping Momma arrange the house and our room and doing our daily chores; making our beds, dusting, and doing dishes (I had to stand on a stool to reach the sink at this time). Sissy and I took turns washing and drying, and when we finished, it was outside to play.

At first, things were ok, on the surface at least – but it did not last long. Within a few short weeks of moving back to Iowa, Daddy was drinking and angry again. We could see a change in him. This time it was different somehow, it was worse than before. His demeanor was gruff, and he would blow up at everything. I can still hear him yelling at Momma. He took his anger out on us girls as well. All of us were afraid of him when he was in his angry moods; it felt like we were walking on eggshells trying hard not to make him mad.

Everyone knew Daddy had a jealous streak when it came to Momma. In my opinion, she was beautiful and not just from a kid's perspective because she was my mother. I had seen pictures of her when she was young and recognized her natural beauty. She always took great care of herself and dressed modestly but well. We loved to play dress up with her clothes and high heel shoes. When Daddy was at work, we had happy and peaceful moments, just the three of us. Daddy seemed to be a loner. I do not remember him having any friends other than one or two couples he and Momma used to socialize with occasionally. I just remember his ever-present mood swings and that he mostly kept to himself. Momma was just the opposite she loved to be around people. She always had a smile and lit up the room wherever she was. Momma never knew a stranger.

Supper would always be ready for him by the time he got home. There were many times Sissy, and I would run to our room without eating because Daddy was angry and Momma would bring us up something to eat later. His preferred method to release anger was to hit us with the heel of his shoe or his belt buckle - and if that were not satisfying enough, he would throw us against the wall. We both knew that Momma got her share of his tantrums poured out on her also; we could hear them almost nightly. I never understood why he thought all of us were so bad or deserved this treatment. Momma was such a loving, kind person and mother. I love the way she taught us good manners and to always be polite regardless how others acted. She said that we were responsible for our actions, not the actions of others who may have made bad choices.

The first summer we moved in we got to go to Sunday school. To this day, I do not know how Momma got Daddy to allow us to go but she did, and we fell in love with our teacher. She taught us all the great Bible stories and verses, many of which I carry with me to this day.

When Daddy was not drinking, he would be sullen and quiet, very different. He would take us out for ice cream, and car rides on country roads, looking for old abandoned schoolhouses (there were many in those days). We would have a picnic on the grounds, spreading a big blanket out for our tablecloth. After eating, Sissy and I would play on the swings, merry-go-rounds, and slides. Sometimes it would be difficult to slide down those old slides because of all the rust on them. Momma would always have wax paper along, and she would tear off a big sheet and place it under us as we slid down. After a few passes on the wax paper the slides were good as new – maybe too good and too fast! We would fly down so fast that we could not land on our feet. Momma and Daddy would laugh so hard. She would giggle and tell us to try to land on our feet, which at this point was impossible. So to prove us wrong, (she only did this one time) Momma grabbed a large sheet of wax paper and proceeded to go down the slide. In a few seconds, she was on the ground landing squarely on her backside with a loud thud, sending puffs of dust flying. The look on her face was that of dismay. We all laughed – long and hard. For quite some time after I recall Momma "sitting" very careful, using a pillow for support. She later learned she had broken her tailbone. These fun family times were few and far apart. When we had them, we enjoyed them to the fullest. The car rides and picnics were our means of entertainment since money was not plentiful.

We loved to help around the house. Momma would turn on the radio to country music, and the three of us would clean until the house was spic and span. It was such a treat when Momma took us to town too. We took turns getting something special if it was not too costly. Momma, Sissy and I loved to go "window shopping" as Momma called it. We would go to the best stores and look at their window displays, which always looked perfect whether it was furniture or expensive clothing. It was fun to pick out what we wanted. When Momma was working at the coffee shop on Fifth Street, she would occasionally bring doughnuts home for us as a treat.

Momma was one who always took great care in her appearance, making sure she was well groomed. We loved to watch her do her hair and makeup. She would take special care to cover up any bruise marks, and then put on her prettiest smile. Momma would tell us to do our very best no matter how minor the task and not to do it halfway just to get it done. For when we take care of the small things, the big things will seem easier or take care of themselves. She always told us it is good to look ahead not back. If we cannot see where we are going, the past can stop us in our tracks, blinding us to what might be. *"How precious is Your Kindness O God; Therefore, the children of men put their trust under the shadow of Your wings."* Psalms 36:7 (NKJV).

One spring day Daddy came home in a very good mood telling us we were going mushroom hunting the next morning, which was on Saturday. These were "Morel Mushrooms" sponge-like in texture, and I still like them to this day. In the cool of the morning is the best time to go hunting for them. We drove to the wooded area of the park early that next morning. We could hardly wait to get out and start hunting. Sissy and I darted out of the car and ran ahead trying to be the first one to find the biggest mushroom. Momma and Daddy would be the first to locate them though as they knew right where to find them. There are good memories that I still cherish today. Picnics in the woods with a blanket for our table, roasting hotdogs over an open fire along with marshmallows for a sweet treat (did not know about S'mores back then!) - all good memories. With every happy moment, there was a lingering thought of why these times did not last, why can't our family have more good days than bad days?

Shortly after that Daddy let Momma buy a motor scooter that had a sidecar. We had so much fun riding that thing around the neighborhood and out visiting family with her. Every once in a while, we would take our dog Sonny on our short trips around town. I wanted to have a safe and happy home, as everyone else seemed to. It was a dream that was full of holes for us. I thought if we were just good kids that would make it all better but no matter how hard any of us tried, no matter how good Sissy and I were nothing changed.

A year has passed, and it was now the second summer in our two-story home in Waterloo, I was about seven. Daddy became moodier and increasingly agitated. The twists and turns of life were taking us through darker corridors – a place of new horrors. Daddy's moods were ugly and full of anger. One-night sissy and I were in our room playing, tickling each other, rolling on the bed just having fun. When we heard Daddy tramping loudly up the stairs, we both knew we were in for it. Yanking open the door with one of his shoes in hand, he grabbed me and gave me a couple of hard hits on the head. At this point Sissy headed for the door, he threw me back on the bed and quickly grabbed Sissy by the hair before she could get out the door. Because she ran, she got it worse. The next day I was outside playing with the neighborhood kids, and the boys (being boys) wanted the girls to take our clothes off for "show" and tell. We all gathered along the side of the back porch discussing the request and our compliance, not knowing Momma had been listening by the back door. She came out and said it was time to come in; playtime was over. Once inside, she informed me that little girls do not take their clothes off for show and tell for little boys. I know it was curiosity amongst the kids that prompted our discussion. Momma was quick to say that it was curiosity killed the cat (a favorite saying of hers) and that resonated loudly with me. I decided not to go back outside and started playing with my dolls. My dolls were my "babies." I took good care of them. Momma told Daddy about the "show and tell" incident with the neighborhood boys. She intended to make him aware of what the "boys" were doing, not what I had "almost" done. She could not have known his response was going to be against me and not the boys. A few days later Momma and Sissy went to the store, and I stayed home. I was playing with my dolls and did not want to go, which was a BIG MISTAKE. Daddy came into the playroom and told me that he heard what happened with the neighborhood boys and the "show and tell" request. He had a wire in his hand, and he took me into the bathroom. He pulled my panties down, laid me on my back, and began to whip me in the private area. The stinging and pain was horrible and lasted for days. I was taking baths by myself by then so Momma did not see the red marks and I did not tell her. The marks eventually went away, but I was in total fear of what he had done, so I did not say a word. Fear became my prison. *"He has given His angels charge over you in all your ways."* Psalms 91: 11 (NKJV). I believe this verse reveals God's protective love and I believe it was the hand of God that kept us physically safe and not seriously injured all those years.

Then Dady began to touch me differently - he started touching me inappropriately - where he should not have. He told me it was ok; he was my father. After that, I would always stay away when he was around. I learned to shove my feelings down inside me, believing I was protecting Momma and Sissy. I would be so full of fear I would get sick to my stomach. Momma would put me to bed, give me hugs, patting my head, telling me things would get better - not knowing my awful secret.

The side effects abuse began to take its toll. We struggled socially and had very few friends. We struggled with our lessons at school and learning. It was a miracle that we ever learned anything. And we struggled in dealing with our emotions. It took all the strength we had to make it through one of Daddy's outbursts. Momma and Sissy were my rock though. They kept me from just giving up. At that time, I did not know if Sissy was experiencing the same level of abuse I was. I was so hard for me to deal with let alone talk about, so we didn't. Our focus was just trying to be on our best behavior. Again, I say God was watching over His little girls.

I know now that Momma was very afraid of Daddy, just as we were. She was a brave person and never let anything keep her down. There were many nights we could hear them quarreling. We knew he was mean to Momma and roughing her up yet there was nothing we could do about it. We would hide under the covers in our beds and pray for her together.

We did not know the freedom and security of a loving and caring father. We carried our hurts and fears with us every day, and I know this affected many areas of our life. I recall Momma telling her sister about the school wanting to put Sissy into a special education class called the Opportunity Room. There the teachers could take time to help the students who were at a slower learning pace. Momma allowed the school to put her in this class hoping to help Sissy learn more, which turned out to be a horrible mistake. It created bigger problems as she was teased and bullied unmercifully, making her all the more fragile emotionally. The school also wanted to put me in the same room, but by this time, Momma would not allow it and requested they move my sister back in her regular classroom.

Sissy and I were tiny little girls for our age, mostly because we maintained the premature framework. We both seemed to catch every childhood sickness that was going around forcing us to miss school frequently, making it harder to keep up with schoolwork. With Momma's help and the help of a kind and dedicated schoolteacher, we did ok. She was a wonderful person, and I thank God for putting people like her into our lives. We may have struggled to learn and considered a bit slow, but we held our own. Momma turned much of her attention to supporting our learning and helping us with our homework. The next two years would be much of the same ups and downs. Daddy's methods of abuse would alternate with his moods, and gradually his episodes became darker and darker.

By this time, Daddy was touching and caressing me frequently. I would just freeze and go inside myself when he would catch me alone; I would shut down. Being so young, I guess it was my way of keeping the bad things out of my mind. I always hated it when Momma worked late at the coffee shop. Those were the days we tried to stay outside and play with the neighborhood kids until dark. When Sissy and I were together, he would leave us alone. I always froze in fear when he would catch me alone. Even at nine, I knew this was not the way fathers should treat their little girls. It made me want to run away, but I had nowhere to go.

Momma did not share with her sisters much about our home life; she kept those awful things to herself. She did no support group or the help of social programs like those in place today. There was no place to go. Such problems were not discussed or mentioned. Even though the three of us knew we had a broken family, we learned to stuff our feelings down inside and go on - not let the bad, ugly things get us down. Momma, Sissy and me drew much closer together, but we each had a secret room in our hearts where we hid all the things painful and scary. This dark and hurtful place is locked tightly, and we individually hold the only key. We would, however, put on a happy face and greet family, friends and the world. I think that each of us has our own story. Think about Jesus example in Hebrews 12:3, He held on while wicked people were doing evil things to Him. So, do not get tired and stop trying. Our salvation is great.

The summer before I went into the fourth-grade we moved again. This time to a pretty, little two-bedroom house on the west side of town. It was smaller but in a nicer neighborhood. There were many neighborhood kids to play with as well, and our school was just a few blocks from our house. As we prepared to move, we were filled with excitement and sadness all at the same time. We were sad to leave our friends behind and our little dog Sonny. Momma did not think the new neighborhood and smaller house would accommodate an old farm dog, so she found him a good home with a family that lived out in the country. We all cried when they came to pick him up, we all really loved that dog. He was so much a part of our lives, but we knew we had to look ahead and not at what we leave behind.

CHAPTER 3
Dark Days

Getting settled into our new neighborhood and house took a few weeks. Sissy and I helped Momma as much as we could - mostly by staying out of her way. She quit her job at the coffee shop so she could set up the new house and stay home with us. She was happy with the move, saying it was a step up for us. We made new friends that summer, and it was a summer of new beginnings for all of us - or so we hoped.

Daddy managed to keep a steady job at the local meat packing company. His job was to de-bone hams. It was piecework - meaning the more you deboned, the more you were paid. It was tedious, dangerous work where one could lose a finger or worse if you were not careful. I do remember the steel mesh gloves he brought home from work when he had to replace them. He continued to be moody and irritable, and most of the time we tried to stay out of the way as much as we could. Our days were stressful and full of fear as Daddy seemed to grow angrier and drank more. We could smell the alcohol on his breath almost all the time although we never saw him drink. I wonder how he kept his job. Momma said he was very quick at his work, which was possibly keeping him in favor with company management.

The summer I turned 11 Momma started to let us go by ourselves to the movies on Saturday afternoons. We would usually see a double feature. Sunday's we would go roller skating at the roller rink nearby. During the summer months, one of us would get to spend two weeks at Grandma and Grandpa's farm in Green Castle, Missouri. This summer was Sissy's turn. We were constantly together, so I always dreaded it when she was gone. I looked up to her. She was the strong one, and I was the shy, quiet one. Yes, we would have our spats, but we made up quickly. Just nine months apart in age, we were more like twins.

The time came for us to take Sissy to Grandma and Grandpas. We would spend the weekend there and then make the trip home leaving Sissy there for two weeks of visiting. It was good to spend the weekend at the farm playing with the animals. Grandpa would put the saddle on the old horse and take us for rides. The two of us enjoyed Grandma's homemade goodies she liked to share with visitors. When it came time to leave, I hid my sadness from Sissy; I desperately wanted to stay with her there. This place was free from stress and fear. We all gave hugs, kisses and said our goodbyes. The drive back home took five hours. I would usually fell asleep within an hour or two, which shortened the time for me. I did not get to go to the movies or roller-skating while Sissy was away. Those were activities we did together as Momma did not want me to go alone. I helped Momma around the house and kept up with the daily chores. The weekdays seemed to crawl by, and I was glad to have neighborhood kids to play with at times.

One afternoon Momma left the house to go grocery shopping. I was unable to find anyone to play with, so I went down to the basement to play in the playhouse that Momma had set up for us on rainy days. I was not aware Daddy had come home early from work. He came down the stairs and quietly walked up behind me. He grabbed my shoulders and turned me around. He looked at me very strange; he was angry...yet not. He did not say a word. He pushed me hard onto to the couch, pulled my panties off and got on top of me. Then it happened.

I was crying the entire time, screaming over and over "Daddy, please don't do this it hurts so bad." I was so afraid; I just wanted to hide or run away. I could not understand why he was doing this to me. Afterwards, I felt so ashamed and defiled - my spirit was crushed, and I became sick to my stomach. What did I do to make him want to do this to me, to hurt me so? I felt like I was no longer Momma's little girl. I had a terrible secret that I did not want anyone to know. What would happen if someone found out - would I lose my home and be taken away from my mother? After that, I stayed as close to Momma as I could, not understanding why this happened to me. I was confused and felt so alone. I had lost my innocence, and I could never get it back - I knew it, and my life would never be the same. The days went by in slow motion. It was awful to feel so defiled. I was relieved when it was time for us to go and pick up Sissy. I could not wait to have her back home, as I felt safer with her around. I knew us being together would help keep Daddy away.

Momma's parents, my grandparents, were such kind, loving people. The two of them were strong Christians. We loved going to church with them and enjoyed hearing Grandma sing in her sweet soprano voice. Grandpa always set in the second pew on the left side of the church, which was called the "amen corner." I can still see that that little one-room church with its old potbellied stove (used for heating) sitting on its platform against the wall on the left side. The minister and his family drove twenty miles one way for Sunday church services. Grandma had them come to their place for lunch so they could hold the Sunday evening services without driving back and forth. The Minister and his family were such wonderful people. They had two kids, a son, and daughter about our age. The daughter and mother would take turns playing the piano during the services. Sissy and I became good friends with her. She was a pretty girl who loved the Lord.

Sissy and I loved staying down on the farm - we did not have to live in fear there. We loved to help gather eggs but did not like it when the hens would peck us. Grandma would laugh at us trying to pull the eggs and would tell us to reach under the hen quickly. Somehow, that never worked in our favor, and we usually got a peck or two!

The weekend picking up Sissy flew by, and it was time for us to return home. I was happy to have her home again but sad to leave the farm. Sissy was telling us all the fun things she did. She got into poison ivy early in the week and scratched it in her sleep to the point it made sores. Grandpa had to take her to the doctor. Despite the incident, she did enjoy her time on the farm; it was a special time for her. For me, it was the summer I wanted to forget.

I tried my best to keep out of Daddy's way as much as possible. I managed to keep a smile on my face and put on a good front, but at times, it was a too much to handle emotionally. Thoughts kept going through my mind about why he did this and did I do anything wrong to make it happen and the tears would just flow.

Starting back to school was almost a relief. It was a new grade, new teachers and making new friends. Sissy and I were just a grade apart, so we did not see each other until we got home in the evening. She would walk home with her friends, and I would walk with mine. We would do homework together then help Momma set the supper table. We usually ate quietly so we would not get Daddy upset. We would clear the table, do the dishes, play outside until it got dark, then inside for our bath and off to bed. Sissy and I still shared a bedroom. There were times we would forget to keep our talking (kid noise) on the low side; we would get a little loud, and that would get us into trouble. Momma would caution us to pipe down, and we knew we had better listen because if Daddy came in there, we would be in for it.

In the fall, Sissy and I were able to go to the Cattle Congress Fair by ourselves. It was our local county fair where kids could show the animals they raised (cattle, hogs, chickens, horses, etc.). There were all sorts of carnival rides, gaming booths, and fair food too! At the time, we lived within walking distance, and Mom let us walk over on kid's day. We would get our treats and ride on the rides until our money was gone. At the end of the day, we were tired, happy girls. We liked to play outside in the chilly fall air. This time of year our best entertainment was outside games. We rode our bicycles and played in the park close to our house. We had set times to play outside, then had to be inside by eight or dark, if that came first. However, on a school night, our homework always had to be done - if it was not there was no playtime.

By the time Halloween came, Sissy and I were looking forward to trick-or-treating with our friends, but we had to stay in our neighborhood. There was always one house that was dark and spooky. We would run up and knock on the door and then run away fast, thinking we were brave. I think almost every neighborhood has that one house kids find a little scary! Momma said this would be our last year to trick-or-treat, as we were getting too big.

I cannot remember what our costumes were, but I do recall we got so much candy it took us weeks to eat it all.

Now that we were a little older, we could stay up later too. We listened to our radio programs every night, laying on the floor in the living room with our ears glued to shows such as Amos and Andy, Roy Rodgers and Dale Evans - and then we would head off to bed. Televisions were just coming out, and most families could not afford them, our family included. We did have some pretty cool records to listen to though (vinyl records, not CDs). We never were able to have friends overnight nor did we stay with any of our friends overnight. We did not even give that a thought, as we had never done that

As the year was winding down our thoughts turned to the holidays. We started saving our allowance and turning in pop bottles for the deposit money so we could shop for Christmas. We would pool our money together for a gift for Momma. We would be very secretive, yet Momma would playfully try to prod out of us what we were getting her for Christmas. Christmas was my favorite time of year. I loved the sounds and carols, the pageants at church, and of course all the Christmas goodies to eat. Momma made the best divinity candy and fudge I ever tasted - and the best cookies. She had a great teacher; her mother was a great cook herself. Our Christmas tree was neatly covered with multi-colored lights along with glass ornaments and icicles. Sissy and I loved to put the icicles on the tree.

This time of year, we would be on our best behavior, and Daddy seemed a little less angry during the holiday season. We still stayed out of his way though. We loved to play in the snow, building forts and making round fat snowmen. We made plenty of snowballs to ensure our fort remained heavily armed for battles with the neighborhood boys. It would always be the girls on one side and the boys on the other. Sissy was a dead shot with a snowball; the boys could not get the best of her. The rest of us did our best to simply keep them at bay. After our snowball battle, we would return to the house for hot chocolate and cookies. As I look back, I can see how God gave us the resilience to keep doing our best, not letting the bad things overcome us, physically or emotionally. *"The Lord also will be a refuge for the oppressed, a refuge in times of trouble and those who know your name will put their trust in you. For you, Lord have not forsaken those who seek you."* Psalms 9: 9-10 (NKJV).

We always said our prayers at bedtime and asked God to help us be good. God was working behind the scenes. I can see His hand clearly on us, holding us tightly and keeping us together emotionally. That winter was extra cold, and Momma took us to school nearly every day. One cold, windy morning we were running late. Momma was still in her housecoat and pajamas when she decided to take us to school before she got dressed. She threw her heavy coat over her robe and away we went. I thought she was brave to do that - what if she had car trouble (remember, no cell phones back then). She was one gutsy lady, I would have never tried it, but Momma did, and she got away with it. It still brings a smile to my face when I recall that quick trip to school.

It was such a delight when Momma would share her childhood days with us, which, was not often. She and her siblings walked to school a very long way, during rainy weather, and icy cold winters on roads that were not plowed as they lived so far out in the country. She would tell us about the one-room schoolhouse and of course the boys and girls "outhouses" (Yes, outdoor facilities!) and one teacher for all grades. Momma's parents were faithful and hardworking farmers with no modern conveniences in their home. Because she was the oldest girl in the family, she had many responsibilities. There was not much time to herself, but even after a hard day's work, Grandpa would get out and play with them. I am so thankful for my Grandparents. They gave us a much-needed place of refuge from all the turmoil at home. I do not know if they knew what was going on at our house. They did not talk about stuff like that in front of us.

Winter and spring were creeping by, staying busy with school and homework helped but life was still was a struggle day by day. I could not wait for summer because it was my turn to spend two weeks at my grandparent's farm. It was an escape for me – even if it were only for a little while.

CHAPTER 4
Days of Destruction

It was early 1950; I would turn 12 this year. At the onset of summer, we were looking forward to getting outside without coats, hats, and gloves, but most of all just being out of school! In the back of my mind remained a fear of Daddy catching me alone – it continuously haunted me. I carried an emotionally deep scar. I wondered if Sissy was going through the same thing and was not talking about it either. My heart ached to know but I just could not bring myself to ask or talk about it. I knew that when we were apart the one left alone with Daddy would be vulnerable to his abuse. It was something we never talked about with each other, deep down I did not want Momma or Sissy to hurt as I was hurting and not thinking or talking about it was my way of dealing with it.

I was incredibly excited for school to be out ready to spend two weeks with Grandma and Grandpa! That world was peaceful, and I could trust that no one would be abusive to me. I packed my bags several days ahead of our departure time with great anticipation. The week before we left, Sissy and I spent quality time together playing in the park and with the neighborhood kids. Finally, the time came for our trip, and it seemed to take longer than usual to get there. We knew the wonderful welcome we receive upon our arrival along with the fresh goodies Grandma always had waiting for us. We both loved our Grandma as much as we did our momma. Grandma's hair was coal black with very few streaks of silver. Her eyes were almost as black as her hair. She could sit on it, and she loved it when we would brush it for her. She was tall and thin, and her great-grandmother was a full-blooded

Cherokee Indian. I thought she always smelled like fresh baked bread and cookies, which is the most delightful smell to a kid.

After Momma, Sissy, and Daddy left to go back home that Sunday afternoon, Grandma and I began our chores by clearing the dinner table and preparing the water on the cook stove to wash dishes. There was no running water in the house, so we used tubs of hot water for washing and cleaning (everything). We used one tub for washing and one for rinsing. Grandma would wash and rinse, I would dry and put away, and in no time, the kitchen was clean. We would rest for a bit or take a short nap before evening chores followed by a light dinner, and Sunday evening church services. We were usually back home by seven thirty or eight o'clock and would enjoy an evening snack of Grandma's goodies before retiring to the front room for bedtime prayer. We each would take a turn at saying our prayers - I loved praying together. I often fell asleep before it was my turn to pray and Grandma would gently nudge me; I would say my prayers, then she would help me up the stairs and into a wonderful, huge feather bed. It surrounded me like a big fluffy cloud. I would fall asleep before Grandma reached the bottom of the stairs.

Grandma would wake me up early every day for chores. Getting dressed quickly, I would rush downstairs eager to help any way I could. Grandma would have breakfast ready; we always said grace before our meals. After breakfast and dishes, it would be time to head to the barn for morning chores. I loved to watch Grandpa squirt the cats in their face with cow milk as he was milking them. They would use their paws to wipe the milk off their face then lick their paws, Grandpa kept them busy. One-time Grandpa asked me if I had ever seen the star in a cow's teat before. Of course, I said no, and he invited me in for a closer look. I bent down closely looking very intently at the teat then Grandpa gave a healthy squeeze squirting milk in my face. He laughed long and hard in his deep hardy laugh, and I laughed too – with milk all over my face. Grandpa loved to play funny little jokes; he had a wonderful sense of humor and was "young at heart." He had deep blue eyes that sparkled with joy and love. The days seemed to fly by so quickly – I enjoyed my time with them thoroughly. I also enjoyed helping in the garden and doing the household chores. Every day was busy just being about the work of living. We started and ended each day with prayer, and every morning we would read a passage or more from the Bible after we had finished our chores. I felt a special peace and joy while I was there with them yet my thoughts would take me back home wondering how Momma and Sissy were doing. I would then tremble with fear thinking about what had happened last summer; praying that Sissy would not suffer the terrible experience I did. I would know in a few days as my two weeks with them was nearly over, and I would have to go home.

I do not recall the ride home that year – or who picked me up, mostly because I was terrified to go home - afraid of what I might find there. The ride home was long – but not long enough for me. Not at least when you are dreading the end. As soon as I walked in the door Momma sat me down for a private discussion; it was what I had feared. She told me how Daddy had sexually abused Sissy during the time I was away. I remember being so scared yet so relieved the ugly truth had come out; I thought Sissy was brave for coming forward. I was so grieved that she was abused. Momma told me that she asked Daddy to leave the house and she was filing for divorce. As Momma sat with Sissy and I she drew us close to her and promised, "He would never hurt us again." I could feel her trembling as she held us close. We all sat there for a long time simply holding each other, all feeling fearful...yet relieved Daddy was out of the house.

I unpacked my suitcase in silence. I did not know what to think or how to feel. I was relieved Dad was gone but hurt for what happened to Sissy. I knew just what she was feeling, and yet I still could not share it with her verbally, it was just too painful to even speak of. I had to move on, and I hoped it would be easier now that it was just the three of us.

The rest of the summer, we spent helping Momma with all the housework as she went back to work. Sissy and I never spoke about our own experiences with our dad, then or later in life. It may have been our way of dealing with it, stuffing it down and pushing it aside.

Family members were able to help Momma secure a good job at the meat packing plant processing the pork products. It was the same place Dad worked but thankfully in a different department and building. Their paths would not cross often. It must have been very hard for her getting into a full-time job schedule, supporting two pre-teen girls at home and dealing with the after-effects of abuse. What strength she must have had. I knew she was a strong woman and was no stranger to hard work, but that had to be a very difficult time for her. There were many nights Sissy, and I could hear her crying. We would crawl into bed with her, giving her lots of hugs and kisses. The three of us would cuddle for a little while before finally settling in for the night. The stress of the situation was hard on her. We were free from the source of our pain; we were emotionally drained but physically safe, a feeling hard to describe. Momma had three sisters who lived close by, it was comforting to have family around to help, and I know it was a comfort to her. By the end of the summer, life was settling down a little bit.

Then Dad started to drop by...unannounced.

It was usually after work or on weekends. There were times we could hear Momma arguing with him; each session seemed to be worse. There would be a terrible verbal fight between them, and Sissy and I would stand beside Momma giving her support. She would tell us to be still for fear he would lash out – she did not want us to get hurt again. It would finally end, and Dad would yell and slam the door on his way out.

In additions to his little visits, he started to drive by the house at night with his lights off, turning around, coming back, setting across the street for a couple of hours or more. There were phone calls that as soon as someone answered, there would be a loud click on the other end. A few minutes later, he would be driving by with lights off then park across the street. He studied our routine, the times and places we would go regularly and often showed up at the same place the same time. When we did our weekly grocery shopping, he would always be somewhere around in the store. Momma told us to ignore him, but it was so upsetting to all of us. He was tormenting us. We never knew when he was going to show up. We all were afraid of him... still. We never knew peace with him around.

School was to start in a few weeks, and I was eager to shop for school clothes. Momma would shop for Sissy one week and the following week for me.

Welfare was not common in those days – there were no "wick" programs to help with expenses like there is today. We had to watch our budget down to the last penny. Dad did pay child support, which helped some.

Momma's brother-in-law was a mechanic at a local car dealer and helped her get a good used car. He was good at fixing things, and he helped her keep the car in good running condition. He also changed all the locks on the doors at the house, which was a blessing from our Lord! It was good to know that Momma's family was around to help us. Dad continued to stalk us every night and on weekends. Momma even caught him peeking in the windows of our house at times. He was like a lion stalking its prey; it was such a helpless feeling.

School started, and it was a struggle to complete our assignments as it was hard to concentrate most of the time, but Momma made sure we had a good home environment. We always had good food in the house, and she would bake for us when she found the time. I can still feel all the love Momma poured into us. That will never leave me.

CHAPTER 5
On our Own

Fall came quickly and the holiday season was upon us. We spent Thanksgiving with some of Momma's family. It was pleasant and uneventful. Her entire family had been our support system through everything. Sissy and I were going to babysit for them to earn Christmas money, allowing them time to do their Christmas shopping as well. We also took different jobs around the neighborhood such as raking leaves, folding newspapers for a dime, and other small jobs to earn money. We wanted to give Momma the best Christmas gift we could. We loved Christmas time and decorating the house (something I still enjoy to this day). We would play Christmas music and sing along to our favorite songs as we decorated our house into a Christmas wonderland. Momma had a special attachment to her vacuum. It was a jar like container with a spray nozzle. She would fill it with liquid pine tree scent and spray it all throughout the house and the tree. It was a very lite scent but lasted for a long time. When finished we would have hot chocolate and cookies. The three of us loved for the house to be spic and span with everything in its place -such great memories and precious times.

It was the first holiday there was no anger and fear in the house. Lingering in our thoughts were concerns about Dad though, and what he might do. Momma did everything she could to keep things festive and light telling us to be thankful for all of our blessings.

Christmas day was filled with joy and sadness over the brokenness that Dad had brought into our lives. Momma would say keep looking forward not back. Hold your head up high and be thankful for the roof over our heads, food to eat, and good health. *"Keep your eyes focused on what is right and look straight ahead to what is good."* Proverbs 4: 25 (NKJV). Dad did stop by for a short time bringing our gifts but did not stick around. For a treat, Momma let us go to the movies and skating the next day. We had a two-week break from school for Christmas and New Years. During this time our daily activities were housework and listening to our favorite radio programs because it was too cold to play outside for very long. Momma was usually home by four in the afternoon.

That winter was long and cold, and the snow was piled up high all around us from digging out the driveway and the sidewalk in front of the house. One day Sis and I decided to make a big snowman out front. We dressed him in red earmuffs, a green neck scarf, a carrot for his nose, and big black buttons for his eyes and mouth. We used two twigs for his arms and placed red mittens on the end of the twigs for his hands. He was huge, taller than we were. Momma had to help us put him together. Afterwards, the three of us got into a snowball fight, and then ended up making snow angels. I remember that day fondly and Momma making time to have fun with us, she was always looking for fun things to do.

Dad continued to pester Momma; he never left her alone for long. He wanted Momma to take him back and forgive him – but how could she though after what he had done to his daughters and all the abuse, pain and anger. The times he did get into the house, it was to visit with Sissy and me - so to speak. He was most likely keeping tabs on us rather than visiting. Momma was always there. Most of the time Dad would end up getting mean and loud and argue with Momma. We continued to fear his temper tantrums. He would tell Momma she would never have another man in her life stating that he would see to that. During one fight, he choked Momma until she nearly passed out. I do not recall her calling the police when this took place – I think she tried to deal with it on her own. She would cry at times saying, "He is going to kill us all." She finally started sharing her concerns with her sisters; Momma truly felt that one day he would kill her. We never knew Momma shared these feelings with her sisters; she did not speak to us about these fears. Why would she – it would only add to the fear we continuously carried around. I know that Momma went through such awful things that she could not share with us. She was never one to talk about her troubles to others, except for a few family members. I do not know how she stood up under the heavy burden. It still breaks my heart when I think about it. She would try to give us hope saying that things would get better with time. I wonder if she was trying to strengthen herself. She never let her fears overtake her. She was a strong woman who never knew real peace during these times. That still brings tears to my eyes.

With spring around the corner, it meant we could get outside more. We would ride our bikes, and go for walks with Momma whenever we got the chance. It was during these walks she would talk about what it means to be a good person and tell us to always act like young ladies, stay well-groomed and of course say "please" and "thank you." Momma was a smart, beautiful woman inside and out, and could do anything she set her mind to. Truly an inspiration! On school days, Momma would have our meals ready for us in the refrigerator when we came home for lunch. We would ride our bikes home (Sis always carried the house key), eat, clean up, then head back to school. It was a quick trip but was good to eat at home.

For Easter, Momma said we could get new dresses and shoes. We were so excited to go shopping - we could not wait for the weekend. We had to keep within Momma's budget, but that was all right with us. When it was time to go, we went to quite a few different stores before we found the perfect outfit and shoes. Sis and I were like two little chipmunks chattering with excitement. That day, Momma took us to Blacks Tea Room for lunch, it was the best place in town to eat – at least that is what we thought. It was on the mezzanine of Blacks Department Store, which went out of business long ago. It was a "high dollar" store in its day though. It was such a beautiful day, each of us enjoyed it thoroughly, and beautiful days were rare.

We all looked forward to Easter, Sis and I had the best time decorating our eggs that year. We took the last egg and dipped it in all of the dyes added together. That poor egg was the ugliest we had ever seen – it was a dirty, rusty color, but Momma took it for lunch saying it's what's on the inside that counts. She was so right. When Easter morning finally arrived, we were all dressed beautifully in our new dresses, and it was a warm, sunshiny day with a chorus of birds singing. All of us looked fresh and neat just like the flowers in springtime. Even the songs at church were of joy and adoration for our Lord Jesus, who was crucified and died for our sins and rose again. I thank God for those special days; they leave me with beautiful memories. We had a wonderful Easter dinner at Aunt Jenny's house. All the kids played games outside after changing out of our pretty clothes of course. We were two tired little girls by the day's end. After bath time and prayers with a goodnight kiss to each of us from Momma, Sissy and I drifted off to sleep dreaming happy dreams for a change.

But happy dreams were short-lived. Dad stalked us all the time. I remember one-time Momma went to lunch with him at work to persuade him to leave us alone. She told us how she felt it would be safe to meet him in a common area at work. After getting their table, Dad went to get the Cokes for the two of them. Returning, he sat down and began to act strangely during the conversation. After taking a few sips of her drink, Mom felt a something from the drink rolling around on her tongue. She quickly spit it out and saw that it was a pill of some type. She left the table, Dad, and the conversation and returned to work. She did not know what type of pill it was, but she knew Dad put it in her drink. I think Momma was afraid to call the police as he threatened multiple times to take us all out if she even tried such a thing. We did not know of any special programs that helped abused families or if such services even existed. Our only support structure was family and Momma did not want to involve family any more than necessary, she was afraid for them as well. There was no place to run. Fear once again reared its ugly head. We all were quiet at the dinner table as Momma shared the details of the day with us. We were submerged in our thoughts of what he may do next.

After the lunch incident, Momma was even more on guard. We constantly made sure the doors and windows in the house were locked securely, and we made sure that none of us was left alone. After a while, tensions relaxed, and things seemed to be at ease, momentarily. By this time school was almost out for the summer and I was not sure how we would be safe being home alone all day. Thankfully, Momma made arrangements for us to provide babysitting and do various chores for family members that lived close. The days we were home, we cleaned house and always kept the doors locked. Dad usually was at work during the day, except for a frequent sick day. Momma had a couple of the neighbors keeping an eye on things as well; she became a pro at staying on top of things.

This summer, both of us would go together to our Grandparents for two weeks, which would help Momma immensely. I am sure that gave her relief knowing that her girls would be safe during this time. Sissy and I were so happy to hear the news but somewhat fearful as we did not want to leave Momma alone, yet we knew she had her sisters nearby. It just seemed that when all three of us were together, we would be all right. I do not know what we thought we could do, but we felt like we were stronger when we were all together.

Dad still would make his nightly drive by, then park across the street in front of the house. He would sit there just watching the house. Sis and I never knew how long he stayed there. Momma would tuck us in bed and listen to our prayers. I do not know how long she stayed up after we went to bed. There were times we could hear her on the phone talking to one of her sisters, but could not understand what was said. Sissy and I would cry and pray for our sweet momma, wishing that Dad's torment would stop…for all of us. My heart still aches for what she had to endure.

We had a good routine that ensured our safety and got us to school on time. Each morning Momma would wake us up for breakfast and then she would leave for work. Sis and I would eat, clean up the kitchen, and get ready for school. We left the house around 8:30, making sure we locked the door behind us.

It was just a few days before school was out for the summer and Sis and I felt excitement and fear all at the same time. Momma's whole family helped us in every way they could. We were grateful for everything they did, including taking us down to Grandpa and Grandma's for our two-week visit in the summer. We were unsure of what the summer would bring. Momma always said to look forward to having all of the good things that God has set aside for our future and take one day at a time. I learned to do my best and never quit just because things got tough.

Momma was getting extra work on Saturdays, and the extra work helped tremendously with the expense of raising two pre-teen girls. She always made sure we did not go without the necessities. We had lots of love, and we all held onto the love and encouragement we gave to each other. We were the three musketeers, one for all and all for one!

Sis and I had our bags packed, waiting for Aunt Lottie and Uncle Byron to pick us up. We had said our goodbyes to Momma when she left for work that morning. We hated to leave her, but we wanted to make it easier for her with not having to worry about us - at least for a while. We were quiet on the trip to the farm as our thoughts drifted back over the last year. You could just feel the tension and concern in the atmosphere. I wondered if Sis was sensing the same thing yet we never talked about it. I do not know why we just didn't. As we neared the turnoff road to the farm, Sis and I both were glad to be together. Each of us had wonderful times on that old farm. Our love for our grandparents and that old farm ran deep. As individuals, we simply do not know how precious these things are (family, friends, and helping one another) until after God has called a loved one home. It is then we realize and feel the influence they had in our lives. I do not think any of us can know the total effect we have on others. That is why I thank God for putting the right people in my life at the right time.

We pulled into the driveway, and our uncle honked the horn signaling our arrival. I bolted out of the car quickly - before it was barely stopped! Along with our two younger cousins, we all rushed in to be the first to receive hugs and kisses. It was good to get out of the car, stretching our legs and chattering at the same time. All of us could smell the wonderful aroma of freshly baked goodies coming from the open kitchen windows. There was no air conditioning back then, so the windows were open nearly all summer.

Sis and I helped bring the bags in, carrying them upstairs to the bedroom we shared. We wanted to jump in the middle of the big ole feather bed right then and there - but we thought better of it. Grandpa had just brought in a fresh bucket of water for us to drink from the well outside of the house. That well water was the best tasting water, and it was always cold. We thought it was fun drinking from the big dipper, each taking our turn.

Grandpa and Grandma's house was our refuge for the next two weeks. We spent the rest of the day playing outside and having fun with Grandpas old farm dog and the barn kittens. We were warned to stay up by the house and not to go into the barnyard as the old rooster would chase us and try to peck us and Grandma did not want the chickens running all over the front yard.

Grandma called us in to wash up for supper. We used a pan of water with soap and a towel. No hot running water coming out of a faucet here. The only modern amenity this house had was electricity. After washing up, the pan of water was emptied into the "slop bucket" that sat underneath the washstand, which we emptied at the end of the day. Grandma did have a refrigerator, but she kept her fresh vegetables and potatoes outside in their root cellar. The evening meal was always light, no heavy food, mostly soup and sandwiches, sometimes leftovers from the noon meal, which was the biggest meal of the day. Later we went to the barn to watch them do chores, feed the chickens, gather the eggs, and feed the pigs. Grandma shut the chickens up for the night to keep them safe. After chores, we would wash up again while Grandma popped us all some popcorn. While we were munching our popcorn, Grandpa would play checkers with us. Everyone would take a shot at taking down the checker champ, Grandpa. I believe he remains the champ to this day! I recall that hardy laugh of his and his gentle teasing after each victory.

We had devotional time in the evenings before bed. Grandpa read a passage from the Bible then each of us would say our prayers. Grandma brought up the chamber pot for us in case we needed a nightly bathroom trip, which we left in the hallway. This is what we used should nature call in the middle of the night, so we didn't have to go all the way out to the outhouse. We had a pot to "potty" in! Snuggling down in the feather bed we talked about Momma wondering how things were going at home. As I felt the tears starting to roll down my cheeks, I wished everything would get better for all of us then sleep would finally overtake me.

In the morning we awoke to the sound of the rooster crowing his loudest, getting everyone up to start the day. I think he took his job seriously. We piled down the stairs with our tummies rumbling at the smell of breakfast cooking and coffee brewing. Grandma always cooked a large breakfast to start the day. She said a good meal under your belt was the best way to get a person going. Starting with good food means strong backs and lots of energy to get any job done. After spending a day with family, my Aunt and Uncle left for home after church and Sunday dinner. We generally had fried chicken with all the trimmings for Sunday dinner, including Grandma's homemade fruit pie. The type of pie she made depended on the fruit Grandpa wanted. Grandma had many different types of fruit to choose from since they had their own orchard and many types of berries. Grandma canned all of them except what they kept aside to eat. She kept her canned vegetables and fruit down in the root cellar along with potatoes and onions.

Our Grandparents farm was certainly not modern or up-to-date even for those days, but they managed daily life quite well. The hours they spent doing simple things just for daily living must have seemed laborious to outsiders, but for them, it was a way of life. Canning season required a lot of water to wash and sterilize the jars and get them ready to pack in the fruit. Canning fruit (or anything for that matter) was an arduous task. The process starts with making the syrup for the fruit, then cooking all contents in a large kettle and spooning the final cooked product into the jars. To seal the jars you had to place them into another large pot of boiling water. The pot had to be filled with enough water to go up to the neck of a quart or pint jar and had to hit the boiling point for twenty minutes, and that was for just one batch. Grandma's cellar was packed full at the end of the harvest season.

Most of the days were long and hard, but there was enough energy left to play some outdoor games such as tag, dare base, and hide-and-go-seek after work was done. Grandpa like to play hide-and-go-seek with us. He was always the one who would go hide, and we had to "try" and find him, but he made sure we wouldn't. I laugh at that now when I think back - I know he didn't want to do the finding as he would have to run to catch us. It was much easier finding a good hiding spot and just resting. At dusk, it was time to go in. Our routine would be the same every night, dinner, games, prayers and off to bed. It felt good to end the day – we would simply be exhausted! Sis and I helped with house chores as much as we could. The two of us took turns getting the water in for Grandma. We were her "gofers," as we liked to say. Whatever they needed we would go and get, and they could keep us busy "fetching"!

In the evenings, we would go with Grandpa to get the cows. We had to walk quite a way to collect them, up and down a few hills in the back pasture. Grandpa would point out all the different types of nut trees and wild berry bushes. My favorites were the hazelnut bush, the gooseberry bush, and the hickory nut tree. We learned a lot about the many things God has provided for our nourishment, and we enjoyed the taste of all of his bountiful supply.

On Sunday's we would go to Sunday school. We liked our teacher at Grandpa's church. She was an older woman with beautiful gray hair; we all called her Sister Ishmael. She used little stick figures made of felt to help illustrate the Bible stories. She would place them on a cloth-covered easel and move them around in story form as she spoke. I could tell she loved the Lord and how she enjoyed teaching us these stories.

Sis and I prayed for Momma every night. Even though it was good to be here on the farm and it was such a peaceful time, there was an undercurrent of fear and turmoil going on in both of us. I know my thoughts never strayed too far from Momma, and what was going on at home. Both of us knew that special look when we were thinking of her and how we wanted to be home. I know she was glad her little girls were safe for the time being. At least I would be home for my birthday in July. I was turning thirteen this year on the July 31st, and Sis would be fourteen in October.

During our last week on the farm, Grandpa wanted us to clean out the milking area in the barn for him. This area had about fifteen stanchions (milking stations), and it was in desperate need of a good cleaning. It took us most of the day to clean it as the place was caked in manure; at least we thought it was manure. We started at the worst end working with metal scoop shovels and worked our way toward the door, scooping and scraping and carrying it out. It was hard, backbreaking work but these two city girls did it. As Grandpa let the cows in for the evening milk, we anxiously waited for him to sing our praises about how good a job we did. He had a very strange look on his face while inspecting our work, not a smile or frown but a look of disbelief. After scratching his head for a moment, he thanked us for cleaning off the cow dung…and removing the light layer of cement he had put down to make that area more level. What? We felt so bad – no wonder it was such hard work! I believe it was cracked very bad because of the weight of the cows standing on it that made it appear to be dried chunks of poo. At least when we did a cleaning job, and we did not leave anything that looked much like manure behind.

Our time on the farm went quickly, and we started to gather our things to go back home. Both of us were excited to see Momma again, but we would certainly miss the farm and our Grandparents. They were very dear to Momma and us. Even though Momma's family was large, there was so much love to go around. Momma surprised us and came down with Lottie and Byron to pick us up. It was so good to see her. When she heard of our extra-ordinary barn cleaning skills, she told Grandpa he should have told us about the slab of cement on the floor. Everyone had a good laugh, and all was forgotten because we were so happy to see Momma. Sis and I loved it that she made the trip to the farm. I am sure she needed the weekend off after working so many of them. We both thought she looked tired, but said nothing to her about it, not wanting to discourage her. We knew the weight and the turmoil were taking a toll, but Momma was still a very pretty woman. That night Grandma made homemade ice cream. Sis and I got to help and turned the crank on the old ice cream maker. I remember Grandpa putting the ice cream mix container into a big wooden bucket filled with ice and salt, locking the crank handle in place, then covering it with an old heavy quilt-like cloth. Sis and I would turn the handle until we could turn it no more, then Grandpa would take over until the ice cream was hard enough to eat. It took a long time of turning and keeping ice on top, but that was the best vanilla ice cream I ever ate. We played with our two little cousins while the adults talked. Soon it was time to say evening prayers head to bed, preparing to go back to Iowa that following afternoon. Our sleep is sweet when loving family is all around us. Sis, Momma and I needed these precious times. We drifted off to sleep, hearing the muffled voices of talking below us.

The two of us awoke to the roosters crowing and mooing of the cows and the wonderful smell of breakfast cooking, which set our tummies growling.

We got dressed and quickly went down the stairs to everyone's cheery good mornings. We were two hungry girls filled with the excitement of being with family and joy of seeing Momma again. Sis and I stayed at the house and helped with our cousins while the ladies cleaned up the breakfast dishes. Then we helped get Sunday dinner prepared and ready for cooking after church. All the kids went to church with Grandpa; we loved to sit with him and listen to the hymns they sang. This little church holds precious memories for us; we dearly loved going there with Grandpa. There was just something in the atmosphere that gave you peace. I now know it is the love of God's spirit lingering, reaching out to meet each of us just as we are.

Today, that little church is no longer in use. Our grandfather was its founder. He named it The Church of God's Holiness. That is where my roots of faith started.

We said our goodbyes to everyone at church and headed back to the farm where the smell of fried chicken and fruit pie surrounded the house. Oh, what wonderful aromas drifting through the open windows and the screen door of the porch. I can almost smell them now.

There was sadness in my heart as we left for Iowa - I could not explain it, but it stayed with me all the way home. The trip seemed so long to me, and everyone was very quiet. All the memories of the past two weeks came pouring in – Grandma hugging me smelling like her fresh baked bread and Grandpa's hug smelling like the hay that he had just put down for the livestock. The two of them – loving, hardworking people. It was a summer that remains with me yet to this day. The legacy they left their family was more precious than all the riches this world can ever offer. I gained a deep faith in our God and boundless love and wisdom from all of their years living for God - being obedient servants to His will in their lives. This faith and love can never be lost or stolen; it grows more in me with the passing of time.

CHAPTER 6
The Calm Before the Storm

We were nearly home, and I was thankful for the long car ride to be over. As we pulled into our driveway, I became uneasy, troubled, but dared not speak of it. We put away the clean clothes and put the dirty ones in the laundry basket to be washed. Mom did the laundry because she did not want us to use the wringer washer. We did everything else she had written down for us to do. We were just starting our third week of summer. Keeping all our chores done and then helping Momma with the yard work. We had an old manual push mower to mow the yard; it makes me chuckle just thinking about it. The only thing I can say about them is you definitely got a workout. We helped the family with babysitting when they needed us. It was free babysitting, but it kept us busy. They did give us fifty cents when they could spare it.

It was about this time; Dad began calling the house and telling Mom that he was going to commit suicide. He no longer wanted to live. He would tell her if she would just take him back he would change but we knew that was not true and we remained very much afraid of him. His temper tantrums of the past would not easily be forgotten and all the beatings and how he hated us to pray or even talk about God and Christianity.

I was going into the sixth grade that year, and a little apprehensive about meeting new teachers and classmates, yet excited at the same time. Also wondering how much homework we would get. The rumor was the higher up you went in grades, the more homework you had to do. This year, shopping for school clothes would be a quick outing for us. We knew we could only get the essentials and we were okay with that. I always loved the time we spent shopping with Momma. Once again she would treat us to lunch at Blacks Tea Room. We were so happy with our new clothes we wanted to wear them right away and protested somewhat as we put them away until the first day of school. Dad did help with our school needs from time to time, and he kept up with child support, which helped Momma a lot with the bills.

There was a small grocery store at the end of our block. Momma would leave us money to go and get bread and milk. Sometimes she would give us a little extra to split a candy bar between us. Saturday mornings, we would help clean house, and in the afternoon, we would go to the movies. We saved our allowance each week so we could get popcorn and candy. Sunday morning, we went to Sunday school and in the afternoons, roller-skating. At this age, we eagerly anticipated the weekends, Saturday afternoon movies and Sunday afternoon roller-skating. We made sure all of our work was finished and any extra work we were tasked with doing during the week. We did not want to miss our weekend activities. Our weekends were special - time to do fun things together.

Life was stabilizing somewhat for us. We had a safe routine, and Momma's job was going well. She met a really nice man at work his name was Ned. She had been seeing him for a little while before she brought him home to meet us. Initially, we were a little withdrawn, but as we got to know him better, we liked him. Sis and I thought he was handsome! He seemed to think a lot of Momma, and it was so good to see her smile again and enjoy her dates with him – he treated her like a queen. Sis and I worried about what Dad's reaction to all of this would be. We recalled the threats he made – that if he could not have Mom no one could. It was time for Momma to have some happiness in her life for a change, and that is what Sissy and I kept praying for.

Momma always looked so pretty when she went out with Ned; she just seemed to blossom during this time in her life. I know she was very concerned about Dad's threats, but it did not stop her from reaching out for a little happiness. They had some good talks together about all that was going on in Momma's life and what Dad was doing and saying. There was a deep concern that seemed to overwhelm me at that time. I finally put it to rest after seeing Momma smile as she brushed aside Dad's angry words. Momma had a lot of tenacity; she always said never let what happens to you rule your life - simply look ahead.

Sis and I took advantage of the last few summer days at the park nearby, playing games and riding our bikes, and eating picnic lunches that we had made. There was an ice cream vendor who rode a three-wheel bike in the park every day about 1 p.m. All us kids in the park would dash over with our dimes and get in line. My favorite treat was a Dream-Pop. It was a vanilla ice cream bar on a stick dipped in an orange sherbet glaze - they were good!

Back then, we did not worry about playing in our neighborhood park without parental supervision. Those times are long gone. I wonder if that little park is still there. I remember our street address, and I recently looked it up on Google earth, and the little house is still there! I was so surprised. It looks so small now but appears to be in good shape for being over 60 years ago. We lived there from the summer of 1949 until January of 1952. I can remember the day we moved in. We were so glad to be in our new house, new to us anyway. I think it was around ten years old when we moved in.

Momma would always give us advice on how to be "proper" young ladies. It was important to her that we knew the right way to act and the right way to treat others, regardless of our circumstances. We learned to say please and thank you, to speak softly, respecting our elders, and never to draw undue attention to yourself. Most of all always be true to yourself. Never put on airs or in other words, never think you are better than anyone else is. God makes each of us special and different to His design and purpose. I have embraced these lessons throughout my whole life. Sissy and I both had a hard time with our self-esteem, but Momma's encouragement and love gave us a strong foundation to build on.

This year school was harder for me; I think all that was going on at home may have been a factor. I always tried my best, and I know that Sis did too. We managed to keep our grades at a passing level, which was all right. However, this year Sis and I were in different schools and were not together all the time. There was a lot more homework that kept me busy most of the evenings. Sis had a lot too. She was changing classrooms now, and it took some time to get used to that. It was difficult for her to have different teachers for each subject, but she did fine. It was going to be my turn next year. I came home for lunch, but Sis ate at her new school. I missed our lunches at home together. I was lonely and somewhat scared without her. After a week or two of coming home for lunch, Mom let me take a sack lunch to school. That was so much better. I did not like eating alone.

Dad continued his harassment of driving by then parking and watching the house. Often, he would barge in when he saw we were busy and would tell Momma that he was going to kill himself. He had nothing to live for anymore. I do not remember how, but Momma always managed to get him to leave. At least there were no physical beatings, but many verbal threats. In bed at night, Sis and I would hear Mom on the phone talking to one of her sisters. We would cry and pray for Momma and pray that Dad would give his problems over to the Lord. It was such a helpless feeling, knowing there was nothing we could do to make our lives easier. We lived day-by-day in uncertainty and always aware of our surroundings. We were strong and had a hope deep within us that came from God. I know in my heart that this strength came from God. We wanted our family whole and the horrible past to just go away – but that is not reality. We had to keep looking ahead, holding our heads up high and doing our very best to take each day as it came.

Ned was a bright spot in Momma's life, and we approved of him - he was good to all of us. Momma always looked so pretty when they were going out. Dad never caused a scene when Ned would come to pick up Momma, most of the time he was not around, but we knew he was watching. I think he knew Ned would call the police or even knock him silly being he was a bigger built man than Dad was. In any case, there was never an encounter between them.

Before we knew it, Thanksgiving was here again, and we had another big family get together with Momma's sisters. There was always plenty of food. Sis and I being the oldest would always watch the younger kids while the ladies did the cooking and cleaning. We were glad to help the family. The first snow came right after Thanksgiving that year, and we built our traditional snowman in the front yard. We enjoyed playing in the snow and inevitably, we would end up in a snowball fight with neighborhood kids. We tried to find fun things to do whenever we could. School activities were not something we did too often, but there were times I would take part in singing Christmas carols and doing a Christmas play at school. I enjoyed those type of activities.

In preparation for Christmas Sis and I took on babysitting jobs and running simple errands for our older neighbors to earn money. This year we wanted to surprise Momma with a special gift, just to see a big smile on her sweet face brought such joy to us. We had no idea what we were going to get her, but there was plenty of time to think on that. We already got Dad's, which was a pair of nice men's gloves and a neck scarf. After all, he was still our dad. Even though what he did to us was horrible we had to move on and not let the past keep us prisoners. Not easy for a teenage girl to do. Momma was so right - we must keep looking for a brighter future and know we are going to overcome when we let go of all the bad things.

Just a week before Christmas we were out with Momma finishing up our shopping when she saw this pretty housecoat and slippers. She almost bought them but decided against it. Sis and I had found our gift! We pooled our babysitting money to be sure we had enough – and we did. I got Momma's attention and went off to another counter and Sis purchased the housecoat and slippers and put them in the sack she was already carrying so Momma would not know. Then she came over to where Momma and I were standing as if nothing happened. We pulled off the surprise!

It started to snow as we finished our shopping. As we headed to the parking lot, the wind picked up. We bent our heads down trying to keep our faces safe from the wind's icy fingers. There were no malls back then and no parking garages either, we had to walk quite a distance to get back to our car. We did not mind - we were too excited to notice the cold weather. We wanted this to be the happiest and best Christmas for Momma! Reaching home, we shed our coats and gloves and unloaded our packages on our bed so we could wrap them later. The house looked so pretty with the tree lit and all the decorations out. Sis and I got the cookies out while Momma made the hot chocolate. Momma suspected that we had bought her a gift by the way we drew her attention away to another counter. She was giving us a hard time by trying to guess what we bought her - all the while laughing and smiling. She was just as happy as we were!

By the next day, there was a large blanket of snow on the ground. Snow of this caliber required "special gear" when doing anything outside. Sis and I put on our winter coats and boots and out we went out to shovel the sidewalk and driveway while Momma fixed breakfast. With the two of us working, it did not take long to clear the snow, and in no time, we were back in the house for a quick meal. After breakfast, we wrapped Momma's gift and started on our Saturday chores. To help with our morning chores, Momma put on some Christmas music, and we sang along as we worked. The house always smelled so fresh and clean and looked so pretty. We were the three musketeers, working together. Sis and I loved those times spent with Momma. She was the rock that kept us strong, bringing joy into our lives.

Since it was Saturday, we wanted to get our work done before our afternoon movie. It was best to get there a little early so we could get our popcorn and candy and find our favorite seats. We enjoyed our weekends, and of course, they flew by quickly. With all of our chores finished, Sis and I got ready to go to the movies. A Roy Rodgers and Gene Autry movie was playing at the theater that Saturday. After the movie, Momma picked us up, and we were chattering in the backseat about what we hoped for on our Christmas list. School was already out until the New Year, and we were happy about that. This particular year was special because we pooled our money to get Momma's gift. Dad would be spending Christmas Eve with us at the house. He told Momma he wanted this to be the best Christmas ever for all of us. Sis and I agreed as long as it was all right with her - knowing Momma would be there with us there was nothing to worry about. It is so tragic for a child to fear being alone with their father. That was the harsh reality of it though. Sis and I told Momma that we could handle it just for a few hours on Christmas Eve, which fell on a Saturday that year. We knew it was going to be special yet we also knew there would be tension at the same time.

We helped Momma set the table for the evening meal. Momma baked cookies and made some homemade fudge and divinity for the Christmas holidays. We got to sample a small portion, and it was simply delicious. Sis and I cleared the table and washed the dishes. After laying out our clothes for Sunday school and taking our baths, we would listen to our stories on the radio. Sunday school was all about our Lord's birth and that very first Christmas. I still love to hear about the birth of our Lord, and the three wise men coming to bring him gifts. Our Lord Jesus Christ has given us the greatest gift of all. Forgiveness of our sins and eternal life through His shed blood on the cross for us even though we do not deserve it. *"For God so loved the world that He gave His only begotten Son, that whoever believes in Him should not perish but have everlasting life."* John 3:16 (NKJV).

After Sunday dinner, Momma took us to the roller rink. I requested new shoe skates on my Christmas list this year; I sure was hoping to get them. Sis got a pair of them a couple of years ago. The roller rink was packed since school was out for Christmas break. I guess the parents wanted to get their last minute shopping done and gifts wrapped and under the tree. When it was time to go home, Momma was waiting at the door to pick us up. Again, we talked about our Christmas list all the way home, hoping we would get the gift we wanted most.

We were looking forward to the upcoming holiday but at the same time a little apprehensive about how things would happen. All of us knew how Dad got angry over even the smallest incident. We were hoping that since it was Christmas; Dad would be on his best behavior. That was certainly our prayer. As we got ready for bed that night, Sis and I were deep in our thoughts over what might happen. Dad was coming for supper tomorrow, and afterward, we would open gifts together. I finally drifted off to sleep simply too tired to think about it anymore.

Momma let us sleep late Christmas Eve morning. We woke to a wonderful aroma coming from the kitchen as she was fixing us a very special breakfast. She was in her worn out robe and slippers. Sis and I looked at each other and just smiled. Momma, noticing our big grins, asked "What are you two up to" and of course we replied "nothing" in unison. It was so good for Momma to be home with us and even in her old ratty bathrobe and slippers, she was still pretty.

During the night mother nature had once again spread a blanket of snow over us. After finishing up breakfast, we donned our winter garments and went out to clear the walks and driveway. Of course, we had to throw a shovel or two of snow at each other, and by the time we finished, we looked like two snow creatures. It is no fun shoveling snow if you cannot have a little fun in the process! Momma made us dust each other off with a broom before entering the house. Hot chocolate and cookies were waiting, and the three of us sat down laughing and talking about the joys of the Christmas season. Momma playfully tried to figure out what her gift from us was and we simply told her she would have to wait along with us!

The rest of the day, we spent in preparation for the Christmas Eve events. As the time drew near, we were praying all would go well. Sis and I helped Momma set the table with a beautiful Christmas tablecloth and a small bouquet of Christmas flowers of red and white carnations in the center of the table with a candle on each side. Momma loved flowers. Everything was ready. The dinner smelled delicious. We had Christmas music playing in the background, and everything in the house was so pretty. Sis and I prayed for this to be as beautiful an evening as the house looked.

Dad was on time, his arms filled with gifts. It was good to see him sober, not even a smell of Sen-Sen, which was his go-to breathe freshener when he was drinking. We helped Momma by filling the glasses with water while she dished up the evening meal and Sissy put the gifts under the tree. Mom and Dad talked about their work, weather and things, just small talk. It seemed so strange to have a Dad there and him not drunk and angry. We did not trust him even though he seemed to have a more genteel spirit. After supper, we helped Momma clean the table and do up the dishes.

As the Christmas music was playing in the background, Momma sorted the gifts, saying she wanted us to save some for Christmas morning. Sis and I reluctantly agreed and told Momma she would have to wait until morning to open her gift from us. We both were so excited and wanted to see how surprised she would be. We opened our gifts from Dad. He bought Momma some beautiful jewelry and a sweater. I do not remember the gifts Sis or I got - I find that strange but I guess after all these years it is understandable. Dad liked the neck scarf and gloves we bought him. Momma had bought Dad a new winter coat. After opening our gifts, we had hot chocolate and cookies. Then after Dad left, we took our baths, got ready for bed, and said our prayers. Hopping into bed, we kissed Momma good night. Later that night we heard Momma on the phone with one of her sisters. We could not make out what she said, but the conversation was short – then she hung up and went to bed. Sleep finally overtook our excitement, and we drifted off to sleep.

As always, the smell of breakfast cooking woke us up. We jumped out of bed not taking the time to dressed and went to the kitchen just as Momma was putting breakfast on the table. We each gave her our morning hug and then after saying grace we sat down to eat. I wanted to eat fast but didn't because I knew it was not ladylike. We talked about how quiet Dad was, which surprised us. I guess he did want us to have a good Christmas, ever after all. We finished our breakfast and settled down in front of the tree to open the rest of our gifts. We wanted Momma to open hers first. As she removed the bow and wrapping paper, she was careful not to tear them so she could save them. She said they were too pretty to throw away. She opened the box and removed the tissue wrapping and gasped in surprise. She quickly pulled out the robe and slippers and put them on; she loved them! We were excited to see Momma's reaction to the gift. Her face lit up, and she had the sweetest smile. We knew she wanted to save her money for things that were essential and she rarely bought for herself. Momma was always putting us first. I was glad we used our babysitting money to get the robe and slippers for her. Giving us her prettiest smile, she said she knew something was up a few days ago when we got her distracted while shopping. That smile on her face was the best gift ever. We opened the rest of our gifts, and I squealed with joy as I had got my shoe skates and a beautiful green taffeta skirt that Momma made for me. Sis got her watch and a pretty set of clothes. It was the best Christmas ever. All of us got dressed and spent the rest of the day just being together. We played some card games, ate holiday goodies and drank hot chocolate then went outside to sweep off the light snow that covered the sidewalk. Of course, we had to have a snowball fight. It was so much fun to spend this day with Momma. Between her working full time and Sis and I in school, it did not give us much free time together. As the old saying goes, "make hay while the sun shines" – meaning, make the most of the time you have when you have the time. It was such a joy just to do fun things together.

Momma had to work the day after Christmas. Mary Jane and I slept in late that morning and ate cereal and toast for breakfast. We ate Christmas dinner leftovers for lunch as it would be around 3:30 in the afternoon before Momma would get home. We took the tree down as it was a real tree and it would dry out quickly otherwise. We were glad to have something to keep us busy. There was always enough work to keep boredom at bay for which we were thankful. I was so excited for Sunday to come - I could wear my new skirt and use my new skates. I enjoyed not having to wear rented ones anymore. They never felt comfortable, and the wheels were usually worn out on one side. We skated from 1:00 pm to 4:30 pm and the time would just fly by. Momma made sure we always had a ride home if she could not pick us up.

It had been a good Christmas considering the circumstances of what was going on in our family. Even though Dad was decent over Christmas, there was still an underlying current of fear. Dad knew that New Year's Eve was coming up. He had been asking Momma for a date. She continuously turned him down. We knew Momma did not want to open a door that would bring him back into the house to live - ever again. Besides, Momma had a date with Ned for New Year's Eve and Sis, and I was babysitting that night. Momma looked so pretty as she prepared for the evening events. With a cheery kiss goodbye, they left for the New Year's Eve dance. Sis and I went to a neighbors house to babysit. We took along some good books to read after we put the kids to bed. Most families did not have TVs at that time they were too expensive. We made it home just a few minutes before Momma and was quite surprised at the generous amount of payment we received. I really needed the extra money as I had spent everything on gifts, which in my mind was well worth the spending. Momma bubbled over with excitement as she shared with us how her evening went. Starting with a delicious meal and beautiful corsage Nick bought her. She also shared that Nick was a good dancer! They had gone to the Electric Park Ballroom. It was a very expensive evening of live music and dancing. It was so good to see Momma start picking up the pieces of her life and starting over.

There were just a few days of Christmas break left, and we were ready to get back school and into our daily routines. Do we dare hope for better things to come in the future? We all wondered what this New Year would bring.

CHAPTER 7
Tragedy Strikes

Sis and I were enjoying our last few days of sleeping in; school was starting back on the following Monday. Saturday morning Dad showed up acting strangely. He told Momma if she would go with him out to his trailer one last time, he would never bother us again. As he talked with Momma, I hung his coat up in the front room closet door. One side of his pocket was heavy. It made a clunking sound as it hit the door. At the time, I was not concerned about it. I was listening to the conversation; it seemed like he was serious about stopping all the harassment and moving on, alone. He told us we would never be bothered by him ever again. He was almost forlorn. I never saw him like this before; he was usually so angry all the time. He was almost apologetic. Momma said she was going with him and it was likely to be to talk him out of committing suicide. She finished getting ready, as she had to work later that afternoon. Our Aunt Lottie and her husband were going to pick us up when the movies were over. By the time we got to the theater and stopped to get our treats, the movie had already started. There was a double feature playing. Laurel and Hardy and a Roy Rodgers film. The Laurel and Hardy movie was half over when we got there, and as the Roy Rogers film started, we decided to stay late and see the first half of the Laurel and Hardy film we originally missed - then call Aunt Lottie when we were ready to come home. Just as we were getting into the latter part of the Laurel and Hardy movie, an usher came and asked if we were the Bell girls; he said he had a phone call for us. I took the call while Sissy stood close to me. We were surprised to get pulled out of a movie for a phone call. It was Momma's sister; she said that something terrible had happened and they were coming to get us - we were to wait in the lobby until they came. Fear gripped my heart. I heard myself speaking, but I did not sound like me. I sounded more like a whimpering child. I told Sissy what Aunt Lottie said - we both stared at each other to afraid to speak. We waited in the lobby in silence our thoughts racing through our minds over the possibilities. I instantly thought Dad had killed himself, I just knew it. Time moved in slow motion. I could see the fear in Sissy's eyes knowing she could see the same fear in mine. We still could not speak. Finally, Aunt Lottie and Uncle Byron came into the lobby. We could see she had been crying. I will never forget the look on her face. It was of horror and disbelief. I just knew that Dad had killed himself and Mom was not able to talk him out of it. We rode in silence back to our house. I was wondering how Momma was doing, was she there when he did it. It felt like we hit every red light and fear lingered and I became anxious because no one was saying a word, the had told us anything yet. Everything still seemed to be in slow motion as we pulled into the driveway. There were other family members there at the house, but Momma's car was not there. As we came into our house, we could feel the deep sorrow among our family like a thick black fog blanketing the whole house. We sat on the couch – poised for the news they had to share. With a trembling voice, Aunt Lottie began to tell us…Dad shot Mom to death in his trailer and then shot himself in the head. Both Momma and Daddy were gone.

I couldn't breathe. Disbelief ripped through my mind – the concept simply did not register with me initially. We both just sat in total silence. The tears of grief overtook us. The shock of our momma's death ripped us apart – it was just so overwhelming. Memories of the earlier conversation between her and Dad kept playing over in my mind. She only wanted to prevent him from killing himself – why did we not see that was not his true intention. I just shut down. I felt like I was a couple of steps outside myself. I knew everything that was taking place around me; I just could not or would not allow it to become a reality. I kept telling myself "this is just a very bad dream. I must make myself wake up, and everything will be all right". Momma will hear my cries, come and hold me, telling me it was just a bad dream. That was not the case. The situation was real. Our sweet, sweet momma was gone. Our world was violently torn apart in one single, selfish act.

I do not know how long we were at the house when I heard my Aunt Tess telling us to pack an overnight bag as we were going to go with her to spend the night. I did not know what time it was, but it was well after dark by the time we got to her house. We undressed and got into bed right away. I cannot remember if either one of us said a word to each other that evening, the pain was too great to talk. We did not even say our prayers. When sleep overtook me, my dreams were of Dad chasing us trying to get us to go with him. We were deathly afraid and kept running from him. I awoke with fear gripping me - I laid there afraid to move.

When morning came, I awoke – but was not "awake." We both were like robots, just moving about but in utter silence. I do not remember the day – what we did or what we ate if we ate at all. We got dressed and went back to our house, which now seemed like a place in which we no longer belonged. I walked into Momma's bedroom thinking it would be wonderful if she had just been sleeping late, and I had to wake her up. I would see her sweet smile and feel her hugs and sweet kisses on my cheek. However, her bed was made up neatly as she left it every day. The new bathrobe we got her for Christmas hung on the hook behind her closet door, and her clothes remained neatly aligned in her closet. I saw her perfume and other personal things, and I just wanted to stay there and never leave that room. It was Sunday and by the time mid-afternoon rolled around the neighbors had read of the event in that day's newspaper. Many brought food and their condolences, offering to help any way they could.

The next few days were blurry for us – and remain so to this day. From the day Momma died until her memorial services, I cannot remember really anything that took place. For some reason that remains a blank to me.

Sis and I both thought if we had stayed home, Momma would not have gone with Dad. It was then I recalled the incident with Dad's coat. I suddenly knew it was a gun that made his coat heavy and made that clunking sound as it bumped against the door. Guilt instantly swept over me like a flood. I thought that if I had just looked at what made that noise, I could have grabbed the gun and run away with it, throwing it far away. I just went deeper and deeper into myself, shutting down, turning my thoughts and fears inward, not expressing or speaking them. I had a terrible secret to keep along with the guilt of not thinking quick enough to stop Dad from killing Momma. It caused a deep cavern of painful regret that that would take years to overcome and heal. This guilt and these deep scars would remain a constant part of my early life.

I felt like a prisoner of my thoughts. Where were we going to live? Who would take two half-grown girls? Would we get to stay together? I knew we would never feel Momma's love on this earth again. I also knew that a monster took our momma, but he would never take the love we felt for her, or she for us – or the sweet memories and the legacy of being the greatest mom in the world. Even after sixty-four years, sweet memories of her come to mind, and I still embrace her as the greatest mother of all time.

It was hard to look at Momma in the casket during the visitation service. The funeral home opened up their side chapel so everyone could pay their respects. It was a big service. I remember how long Momma's funeral procession was. It was surely a tribute to Grandpa and Grandma as well as Momma. It was bitter cold that day. Though it all I wanted to scream, I wanted to know why? Why did this happen? She was such a special person. She did not deserve this. I could see the gunshot wounds on her arm even though the funeral home attempted to cover them with makeup. Momma still looked beautiful. She was only thirty-four years old. I know our whole family was in shock and had a level of grief that cannot be described. Unless one experiences grief such as this – the words I use cannot fully describe the fear, anger, confusion, regret, and remorse- the gamut of emotions you experience all at once. It's truly indescribable – especially from the perspective of a young, abused girl.

The family came back to our house to allow us to get more clothes and personal things. This time reality set in - Sissy and I no longer had a home. No more hugs and kisses from Momma. No more shopping trips and having lunch with her. That next day we went back to the funeral home for the final service. There were many people there, Sis and I did not know too many of them. They were co-workers and friends of Momma's. There was a visitation service for Dad that day as well. It was also hard to go up to the casket. I felt such anger. I never knew that type of anger before. You could see where he had shot himself in the right side of his head and where the bullet came out his left eye.

Some of the neighbors were talking about the events with our family nearby. They talked about how Dad showed up the afternoon of the shooting looking for Sis and I. He was asking neighbors where we were. Later, after several conversations with neighbors and family, it was believed that Dad called the police from Momma's house after he shot her. He left Momma dying in his trailer as he drove back to her house looking for us girls. I am guessing it was between ten to fifteen miles one way. Momma was likely still alive when he returned. He gave her a final shot in the top of her head, ending her life. I cannot imagine how she must have suffered. Years later Momma's youngest sister told me that she had gone to the trailer with some other family members to collect some personal items of Moms. She mentioned that upon entering the trailer, she could see blood everywhere. After fumbling through a few things, they found the key to Momma's house covered in blood. Dad had to take it from her to get into her house to find us girls.

Grandpa and Uncle Emmitt were in from Missouri and the funeral director from Queen City, MO came up with the hearse. Mr. Keith previously provided funeral services for other family members and Grandpa made arrangements for Momma to be laid to rest close to his home in Green Castle, MO. After the visitation service in Iowa, our family would go to Missouri for a final funeral and burial.

Grandpa also had Dad's body sent by rail to a Kirksville, Missouri funeral home. Dad's immediate family took care of his funeral arrangements. I do not remember Dad having a service in Iowa, but his family held a small one in Kirksville. I do not know any of the details, but I know that Grandpa paid for the train fare to have Dad's body shipped to Missouri. I believe only a godly man could do that. I cannot imagine the grief he felt as a parent losing a child that way.

After the funeral services, we all went to Grandpa and Grandma's for a while before returning to Iowa. Mom's sisters began to discuss living arrangements for us. Sis decided to sit outside the door and listen to the conversation, but I did not want to hear the discussion. She was listening for the longest time when she finally came over to me and sat down. There was a look of concern on her face. They're splitting us up she said, that was their decision. I was heartbroken at the news. Deep down I think we knew of the possibility of this happening as all of them had young families of their own. It was still a hard pill to swallow. We were still in the same town at least, but it meant a change of schools for both of us. As far as I could see, the future looked bleak. My grief and anger were overwhelming. I couldn't cry and I had no one to talk to about my feelings. I was going in slow motion as if I were watching from the outside but not participating in life. The guilt of realizing that Dad had the gun in his coat pocket that dreadful morning along with the anger and grief of what happened was too much to carry at times. I knew I had to go on and be strong, but I continued to stuff my feelings down deep, not wanting to feel the pain.

I remembered what Momma always told me, "Always look forward to the future - there are brighter days ahead." How could there be bright days without Momma, and not having Sissy close? Our lives were turned upside down in the blink of an eye. Finally, they all came back downstairs telling us what we already knew. As I stated earlier, it was a hard pill to swallow, but we knew we did not have any say in the matter.

That following day we went back to Iowa. As we pulled into our driveway, I wondered what was going to happen to our house and all our things. It was still a week before we started back to school – in our new schools. The family decided to rent Momma's house out furnished, making it easier for everyone. All of our things we did not need were stored in the attic temporarily until better arrangements could be made. As Sis and I were gathering our clothes and other personal belongings, we just hugged each other, not saying a word. Turning our backs on our little house there and stepping into an unknown future. Only God knew where we would go from here.

Sissy and I never got a chance to know our mother as a woman. We would have learned so much from her. There is nothing like a mother's love to keep you secure. Knowing that helped keep us going and we were determined to make her proud of her little girls.

Waterloo Sunday Courier
FIRST WITH THE NEWS

WATERLOO, IOWA, SUNDAY, JANUARY 8, 1951

SLAYS DIVORCED WIFE, THEN KILLS SELF

Victims of Double Shooting Yesterday

Shown above are the bodies of Eldon Bell, 37, and Velma B. Bell, 34, following a fatal shooting yesterday afternoon in a small trailer two miles south of Waterloo on highway 218. Dr. Paul O'Keefe, deputy county coroner, is shown examining the bodies. Both Black County Sheriff H. E. Wagner termed the deaths murder and suicide. The Bells, parents of two daughters, were divorced last summer.

TWO CHILDREN LEFT ORPHANS BY SHOOTINGS

Eldon Bell, 37, Murders His Ex-Wife in Trailer Home on 218.

A father of two children shot his divorced wife to death and then killed himself in his small trailer home two miles south of Waterloo on highway 218 yesterday afternoon.

Sheriff H. E. Wagner said Eldon Bell, 37, shot and killed his estranged wife, Velma, 34, and then committed suicide.

The couple, divorced last summer, leave two daughters, Mary, 16, and Mae, 13.

Both girls had been living with their mother at the Rabo' avenue, in a home their parents had been buying before the divorce.

Wagner said that Bell had been urging his wife to reconcile but that she refused.

Recensntact Call.

Early yesterday afternoon Wagner the police received a telephone call from a man who said he was Eldon Bell.

The man told police to come to his trailer, that something "terrible had happened."

Police drove to the scene but when they got there Bell and his wife were dead on the floor of the trailer.

Wagner summoned Wagner to take charge since the trailer is located about two miles outside the city limits, just off highway 218 south.

Wagner investigated the scene and 'pronounced the deaths a murder and suicide.

Bell pumped six slugs from a snub-nosed, .32 caliber revolver into his wife's head, breast, side and right leg.

Wagner found nine empty cartridges in a waste basket in the trailer.

Apparently Bell reloaded the gun with nine slugs and then shot himself through the right temple.

Only one cartridge in the gun had been fired when it was found in Bell's right hand.

Wagner found the bodies lying on the floor of the trailer, Mrs. Bell underneath her ex-husband who was lying on his back near her body.

She was partly clothed in a sweater, pants and brassiere. Bell was fully clothed except ing for a shirt.

Bell apparently had covered his dead wife's body with a pine coat she had given him at Christmas time.

Reconstruct Crime.

Wagner said he believed that Bell murdered his ex-wife, covered her, drove to a telephone, called police, drove back to the trailer and then killed himself.

Relatives told Wagner that Bell was in love with Mrs. Bell but that his efforts to win her back failed.

Apparently the climax to the marital trouble came Friday night when Bell asked his wife for a date. She refused, Wagner said, because she had a previous engagement.

Later, Bell made a call to the Rev. Paul Davis to discuss his personal life.

Yesterday Mrs. Bell telephoned Rev. Davis to talk about her ex-husband's attempts at reconciliation.

Neighbor Saw Couple, Wagner said he didn't know

See **MURDER**
Continued on page 14, col. 1
* * *

Eldon and Velma Bell are shown above in a happier time. Their lives ended yesterday afternoon when Bell shot Velma, his divorced wife, and then himself.

MURDER
Continued

how Bell got his ex-wife to consent to go to the trailer yesterday morning.

A neighbor, Vernon Sawvell, who lives in an adjoining trailer, told authorities that he saw the couple go into the trailer just before noon yesterday.

No one reported hearing any shots or arguments.

One neighbor reported that Bell had been living in the trailer about two months.

It was reported that Bell often saw his ex-wife since their divorce.

Deputy County Coroner Dr. Paul O'Keefe said Mrs. Bell died of multiple gun wounds from body to head.

A partly-filled pint of whisky was on a small table in the trailer.

The bodies were taken to O'Keefe & Towne funeral home.

Came Here in 1946.

The victims of the tragic episode came to Waterloo in 1946 and both had been employed at the Rath Packing Co. Mrs. Bell for a period of six months.

Born Nov. 6, 1917, at Greencastle, Mo., Mrs. Bell was one of a family of 10 children born to Mr. and Mrs. Thomas Billington.

She resided at Greencastle for a number of years and attended school there. Her marriage to Eldon Bell took place in May of 1936 at Greencastle.

Soon after their marriage they went to Wyoming where they farmed as homesteaders near Cheyenne for about three years prior to coming to this city.

Surviving Mrs. Bell besides the two children, Mary, 16, and Mae, 13, are five brothers and four sisters.

CHAPTER 8
The Aftermath

My Aunt Jenny had my room all ready for me. As I walked into that tiny bedroom, I felt like an intruder entering into a strange land, unfamiliar with my surroundings, all alone and without my sister. It was at this point I knew I had to grow up. Squaring my shoulders, remembering Momma's words - never look back, look ahead and take one day at a time. There will be better days ahead. That is what I kept telling myself.

Aunt Jenny and Uncle George had a two-year-old boy. Very cute and very full of energy. I felt like I could be of some help to the family by watching him. I was thankful I had a place to stay and praying time would help my aching heart. I was to start school in a few days, and I knew that would be quite an adjustment not knowing anyone or the teachers. I felt like I had moved to a new country and did not know the local language. Overnight I left my childhood behind. I knew I wanted to make Momma proud of me and I vowed that very day to do the best that I could do. I would work hard helping my new substitute family out - wherever they needed me.

The next few months were rough, trying to do school work, helping where I could at home and dealing with grief, anger, and guilt. I never talked about it, just kept stuffing it deeper, refusing to deal with it. I just knew it was too painful to try to sort through it mentally and I had enough pain to last me a lifetime. My Aunt and Uncle did their best to help me adjust; I just wasn't getting there. I did some babysitting for the neighbors on weekends, but I desperately missed Momma, Sissy and our weekend routine of movies and skating. My new skates were still in the box, and I only used a couple of times.

I did wear the green taffeta skirt that Momma had made for me. I still went to the same church and thankfully Sissy' did too. That was the only time we got to spend together. I was getting into a routine, but I had a broken heart that was too tender to make new friends at school. I finally made a friend of a girl in my class, and she and I became close, which helped some. I was still so unhappy and sad - I constantly carried the weight of guilt, anger, and grief for the loss of Momma. The loneliness seemed to overtake me, and the awful reality of life without my loved ones was too much to bare at times.

Aunt Tess noticed I was having a hard time dealing with all the changes, yet there was little they could do, having a small child of their own to care for. They decided it would be better to let my Uncle in Missouri take care of me. All of his stepchildren were grown, and he and Momma had always been very close. They thought he could give me the special attention I needed. So it was decided I would finish out the school year with him in Missouri. I was in the sixth grade. I think they wanted to give me the support I needed and felt it was important for me to be in a less stressful place. It was another hard pill to swallow, but I could not blame them. They were dealing with grief and a baby, adding an emotionally struggling pre-teen girl was likely more than they could handle. All of us were trying to adjust to such a tragic loss. By the end of the following week, I was on my way to Missouri. I could not think or feel anymore because the emotional pain would run rampant. I was determined to keep a strong upper lip in making the best out of a bad situation. Like Momma said, never give up, never quit, always look for the silver lining in every cloud. But this cloud was dark – and had no lining

Driving to La Plata, Missouri was a long trip even though we met my uncle at Grandma and Grandpa's farm and drove from there. I did not know what was ahead of me. My uncle asked me why I was so quiet and all I could say was that I was tired. He was a nice man and told me how glad he was to be able to take care of me. He loved Momma dearly. He married a lady who was previously married and had two children. Her kids grew up with my uncle as a father figure. His wife was a very short woman, a little on the brash side, not at all a genteel woman like Momma. I could feel her resentment upon my arrival. I could see it in her eyes. Laying in my bed that first night, I felt the hot tears start to flow. I brushed them away and said to myself, stop it. Grow up. Do not make it worse.

That first week or so was ok; I did what I was told and kept to myself. I had to ride the school bus because my uncle's house was way out in the sticks, no indoor plumbing or water, just a well alongside the house. Here, I was totally alone – not even living in the same town as my sister anymore. I missed her so very, very much. By this time, I had stopped praying at night.

I shared one large room with two beds with my Uncle Greg and Aunt Lacy. I was so mixed up inside to the point of not caring what happened to me. Life was just so hard, and I felt so unwanted, alone and frightened about my future. Even though I always did what I was told, that did not seem to be enough for my Aunt. She found fault in everything I did, telling me I was too stupid to learn anything.

On Saturday nights, we would go into town for supplies. All the local farmers and families would gather together in the town square park and sit and chat about their week and how crops were doing, and of course about their kids. Not knowing anyone, I would sit quietly, say my hellos and smile. People seemed to avoid me though, and I could not understand why. They would look at me, shaking their heads. It felt like they were treating me as if I was an idiot. Because Momma taught me to be polite, I would smile and say the cheeriest hello I could. Then they would give me this hideous smile and keep walking. I fought back the tears, determined not to let them see me cry. It frequently happened, nearly every time we went into town. Then, one day I overheard Aunt Lacy her telling a group of ladies she was speaking with that I "wasn't all there." I was crushed...it took my breath away. All I could do was withdraw even more. I could not understand why a person would treat another person, especially a child who had been through what I had been through - in such a manner. I had never done anything to cause her such resentment. I felt so alone and lost at that time. My heart ached for Momma and Sissy. I kept thinking it has to get better. I am with family. I prayed for the hurt and rejection to go away.

School was letting out for the summer, and I somehow managed to pass the sixth grade. I was afraid what spending an entire day on my Uncle's farm would be like. It was a small farm. They milked a few cows, had a few chickens and managed a fairly large garden, which I helped maintain. While they were out doing morning chores, I would do up breakfast dishes, make beds, sweep the floors and dust. Sometimes in the early afternoons, we would visit some of their neighbor friends. I never really had anyone my age that lived close enough to play together.

I loved to read, so when we went into town on Saturdays, I picked up some books at the small library in town. I did a lot of reading, which helped my emotional status a great deal. This summer I was to turn fourteen. School let out at the end of April here so the kids could help with the plowing and planting of crops. That community was mainly farmers. I did get to see a few classmates in town on Saturdays. We usually spent time in the drug store sipping a coke or a malt.

At summers mid-point we went to Grandma and Grandpa's farm for a visit. It was so good to see them. I just adored them. Grandpa and Grandma came out of the house to meet us. What a joy it was to hug them and get big warm hugs back. I could not stop the tears from rolling down my cheeks even though I held the audible sobs back. We all gathered around the table for some fresh lemonade and sandwiches to tide us over until the noon meal. I had quickly brushed the tears from my cheeks before entering the house. After eating my sandwich and chugging down my lemonade, I went outside heading toward the barn to find the new litter of kittens Grandpa told me about. I loved animals, as did Momma and Sissy. We did not have a pet in our house with Momma though. I went up into the hayloft, and there were five of the cutest little kittens all curled up, sleeping in the loose hay. I love the smell of hay. It brought back memories of my summers spent there in the past, along with a joy to my spirit that I had not felt in a long time. The fruit trees in Grandpa's orchard were in bloom. The sweet smell of the blossoms was great. It was the first time I had smelled their aroma in a very long time. I just sat there holding one of the kittens, enjoying the precious memories of summers past. The sounds of the cackling hens and the animals below me snapped me back to reality. I put the kitten back with the others. Going back down the ladder, I kept telling myself how I must keep looking ahead, doing my best each day. Even though the road is rough and rocky, I would not give up. Quitting was not an option. I did not realize it, but my God was giving me His strength and working behind the scenes on my behalf. When I returned to the house, I could tell they had been speaking about me. I do not know how...I knew it. My Grandpa asked me, was I happy staying with my uncle? I guess the look on my face told him what he wanted to know - but I did speak from my heart when I answered no. I missed seeing Sissy.

With that, arrangements were made for me to move back to Iowa; I was to move back in with Aunt Tess and Uncle George where I started; they were coming to get me that next weekend. I was relieved really, it seemed like a heavy load had lifted from me. I knew that my Uncle's wife had a lot to do with the change; I knew she wanted me to leave. Years later, I would learn that some people believed my Uncle was a harsh man in raising his stepchildren. Living there was hard for me, but I did not experience any harshness from my Uncle. I guess that is why his wife disliked me so - she was getting back at him at my expense. I will never know.

By the following weekend, I was on my way back to Iowa – move number three. I was so glad to be going and that this chapter in my life was behind me. I knew my uncle felt sad, but he understood, and I have since forgiven his wife. I never knew what she went through in her life that caused her to be so bitter. Now that I am an adult, my feelings for her have changed. Forgiving her set me free from anger and resentment.

I was so excited and looking forward to seeing Sissy again; I could hardly contain myself. This fall I was moving up to Jr. High so going to another new school - McKinstry Junior High. I would be starting the seventh grade, and I would be in a different classroom for each subject. This routine would be different for me - it was the first time I had to change classrooms for each subject. I was looking forward to living in Iowa though and having running water inside, both hot and cold and inside bathrooms and tubs. Most of all, for getting out of a situation that simply was not good for me. It was a beautiful ride back to Iowa. I was full of questions. How was Sissy? When would school start in the fall? Were there any new kids my age in the neighborhood? Had they sold our old house yet? I finally settled down and slept a bit, awakened only by the car slowing down for a stop sign or light. We were going through town, headed out to my Aunt and Uncle's place. I was nervous but glad to get out of the car. I made a mental note to myself to do the very best I could, hoping it would work this time.

The summer went fast. I kept busy, helping Aunt Tess clean and watching my cousin off and on and I made a little money babysitting. I did not get to see Sissy that much as she also was busy with her summer job. That summer I turned fourteen. My Aunt Tess baked a cake for me and made me a nice birthday dinner. I do not remember if Sissy joined us or not. We were past doing fun "kid" things together anymore – we left all that behind. Sissy – Mary Jane – was busy with her life and I was busy just to hold on. I was still grieving Momma. It seemed that no one in the family would talk about what happened. It was considered "taboo" to even bring up the past at least with Sis and me around. I think also it was too painful to talk openly about and most of us did not know how to deal with the pain and torment of what happened.

We went shopping for school clothes later that summer. I remember we had to have gym shorts and blouse, white tennis shoes and socks and a one-piece swimsuit. The school was newly built, brand-new, and about eight blocks from my house. A nice park was halfway in between my house and the school. Some of the kids would stop there on the way home from school to play ball or just to hang out. Just before school started, Momma's house went up for sale, along with some of the furniture. That day was sunny and warm. I remember Mary Jane and I sitting on the living room chair and couch out on the front lawn in the yard sale. It was like the door to the past was going shut. The yard sale took care of most of the household things, and the rest went to Goodwill. I think everyone was glad when that sale was over. Sis got to keep her rocker and a few other things, and I got Momma's cedar chest. When we went to remove our belongings left in the attic, all of the personal keepsakes that Sis and I wanted to keep, they were gone. The people who had rented the house had taken everything. We were devastated – how could people do such a mean thing. Sis and I may have lost our home with Momma, but we will carry all the memories, good and bad, the rest of our lives. *"The*

Lord is my light and my salvation; Whom shall I fear? The Lord is the strength of my life; Of whom shall I be afraid." Psalm 27:1 (NKJV).

Just before school started Aunt Tess took me to get the schedule for my classes and my homeroom number. It was a neat school. I was looking forward to going. I got up early the first day, wanting to take my time in getting ready to look my best, and I was not sure of how long the walk would take me. I had written my locker number down, not wanting to forget it. The building was new to everyone, so we all had to learn our way around. Thank goodness the teachers had their names on the doors! It was a great experience for all of us. The first couple of days, there was light class work. All the teachers were nice. I had my first male teacher. He was good at giving us a ton of homework, which we all complained about. His class was my homeroom. We started our day with his class every day. It did not take long for me to make new friends. It was good to get back to school, and back in Iowa. I enjoyed swim class but did not care for gym that much. As the school year progressed, I continued to make new friends. I did not get to have friends overnight, and I did not get to spend the night with a friend, it was not allowed. My aunt and uncle did everything they could to help me adjust. Mary Jane and I did not get to see each other too often. She was now going to school across town from me. I was hard to get time together, but we did manage to do an hour or two once in a while.

Life was so different for both of us. The three musketeers were no more. It still brings sadness to my heart knowing that Sis was going through the same thing I was and we could not talk about it with each other. When the memory of that awful day pushes its way into my mind, the guilt would overtake me, thinking why did I not know that heavy object in Dad's coat was the gun. That was why his coat pocket was heavy, clunking as it bumped against the closet door. As the tears would start to roll down my cheeks, I would quickly brush them away and remain determined to keep my composure around others. I would push that thought back into my hidden place. Going on to do the task at hand the very best I could.

Summer turned to fall, and Thanksgiving was fast approaching. We were spending this holiday with my uncle's side of the family, at the request of his parents. All of his brothers and their families were going to be there. I was a little nervous, I had not met any of them before, but my uncle put me at ease joking with me saying, "They don't bite until they get to know you." He loved to tease.

Uncle George and Aunt Tess were strong Christians. We would read a few passages from the Bible and have prayer every night before going to bed. I know they were doing their best. I am sure it was hard being a young couple with a small two-year-old and a young teenage girl who was not their own. It was a great responsibility I know, and I am truly very thankful for their commitment.

Aunt Tess let me help her make the food along with some candy to bring to our family Thanksgiving feast. It was fun getting to do things like that with her; we made several side dishes to go with the turkey. She was a very patient and loving person. I loved her zeal for the Lord. She had a strong influence on me; she was my idea of what a Christian should be. Our Thanksgiving dinner was great. I fell in love with my Uncle's family. They were beautiful people. All of the women were great cooks. I especially fell in love with his sister. She was such a sweet woman. His two brothers were full of humor, just as he was. I have great memories of that day. It helped me realize I do have a family who cares. Even though no one can love you as much as a mother does, family can come alongside of you and give you the support you need.

These were my teen years when I needed my mother though. It was a daily adjustment not having her there and knowing that she was not going to be there for important things to come. Occasionally something would remind me of her, a word or an action from one of her sisters and I could not keep the tears back - I would just go off by myself for a while. It was getting close to a year since that evil day, and I knew I needed to keep looking forward even though doubts kept haunting me of how will I ever make it without my momma. I managed to keep busy at school with homework and with church choir practice for the upcoming Christmas program. I still did not get to see Mary Jane enough, and I wondered how she was doing. I wonder how she felt about us not having that closeness we once had. When we did get to spend some time together, it was very short moments, and those were few and far between. Both of us did babysitting on weekends and other school or church activities, our lives were changed forever, and we were starting to go in different directions. We were growing into young women wanting to stretch our wings and see how far we could fly on our own. That time was still a little way off. It is truly sad how life can tear people apart, leaving a hole where there was once a close relationship. I have since learned you can still have a good relationship even though you're not with one and other all the time. I have good memories of us as kids doing fun things together. How we comforted each other during hard times. I would cling to those thoughts often as we went our separate ways.

With Christmas quickly approaching, my thoughts took me back to the last Christmas we had with Momma. How Sis and I worked to save our money to get Momma's Christmas gift not knowing it would be the last Christmas we would have with her. I continued to babysit around the neighborhood for a little spending money and helped the family by watching my cousins off and on. Aunt Tess did not decorate the house for Christmas quite like Momma did, though it was wonderful to me. I also missed our special shopping times and the lunches we had with Momma. I think of how she would teach us how to act and walk as ladies who dressed neatly and was well groomed. Tess was also as neat as a pin. She also took great care in keeping her home neat and clean. I remember times her little boy loved to get out all of his toys and string them all over the house along with cookie crumbs. She would look at him and smile, calling him her messy little boy. It was at that time she was expecting her second child. I was so happy for her. I know she and her husband wanted a big family. I helped my Aunt Tess clean house and watched their little boy when she was not feeling well. It was good to be with a family who cared about you. Life has a way of moving forward regardless of human tragedy. We learn to trust in God to bring us through those times of devastations stronger than we were before. I know without my God on my side I would have fallen through the cracks long before.

The closer it got to Christmas the more depressed I grew. Unable to see Mary Jane for long periods of time was beginning to take its toll on my emotional status. I knew this Christmas, our first after losing Momma, would bring all the memories rolling back. Some good but many filled with tragedy. I was also still emotionally reconciling my time in Missouri, I knew I had to put it behind me, but those negative thoughts and feelings seemed to hang in the corners of my mind. I kept telling myself over and over that it was time to move on. Each family member was dealing with the loss of Momma the best way we could; we had to take it one day at a time. I've heard it said that time heals all wounds and it is true for me today, as a young teenage girl though time was not helping much.

School was going well, and I liked Junior high. I sang in the choir and enjoyed watching sports. Sometimes I would watch the cheerleaders practice a little after school, but not for too long because I needed to get home to help there. I always took my lunch, and I would save the cookie for my little cousin. He would come running down the road as fast as his little legs could carry him to get his treat and hugs. He was such a cute little guy. When I was a few steps from the house, I would see my Aunt open the front door and him running to me with a boyish giggle, wanting his treat and hug. After supper and homework at night, she would let me help her make cookies and homemade candy for the upcoming Christmas season. She was a good cook I do not know how much help I was, but I enjoyed doing things with her. .I still love the smell of fresh baked goodies and the good feeling of togetherness with family.

I do not remember going Christmas shopping that year, or if Sis and I exchanged gifts. I do not remember the events of that Christmas at all, not even what gifts we exchanged. I guess because of the grief I was going through at that time, or maybe it has just been too many years since then. I do recall, however, a deep, deep sorrow every time I thought of Momma's sweet face as she opened her gift from us.

I babysat for New Year's Eve and stayed well after midnight once again. The family lived just a few houses from us in our neighborhood, and they had all girls. I babysat there often, so the girls knew me. The oldest girl helped me a lot. They were good kids. The going rate then was a quarter an hour, and after midnight, I would double it. I thought it was good money. Likely, very different from what babysitting jobs pay today.

January 5ᵗʰ came – it was the one-year anniversary of Momma's death. I struggled to keep my mind occupied and stay busy, as did the rest of our family. I often cried – wounds only partially healed felt as if they burst open again. I had school that day, and it was hard to concentrate in the classroom. I had to fight back the tears multiple times thinking that the day would never end. I was so glad to hear the school bell ring signaling the ending the day.

After dinner that evening my aunt and uncle sat down with me in the living room, the little one was down for the night. We talked over our feelings. It was a very rough time, but I do believe God was there in it with me. I realized they had feelings of hurt and anger as I did – feelings they struggled with often. We all cried, and then we prayed together for God's strength and His love to bring us through these terrible days. I felt closer to both of them after our talk and prayer time. I know without God working behind the scenes, we would be bitter people. *"Yet I will not forget you. See I have inscribed you on the palms of My hands. Your wails are continually before me."* Isaiah 49:15-16 (NKJV).

As I look back on those broken days and the deep, deep grief our family felt, I am thankful for a godly family who pulled together to bring Sis and me to a stable environment. Yes, there were mistakes, but it is through those mistakes that we grow. Giving God our brokenness, He, in turn, will help us have a beautiful, strong life in Him. His Love will heal us, turn things around and heal our brokenness. We must first allow Him to have total access to our lives. It is not for us to see the future. It is our job to put that into our Lord's hands and to trust him with all of our heart.

I was busy the rest of that month helping Aunt Tess as she started having bad migraine headaches. She would get so sick from them my heart went out to her. The little one was a busy little boy. When he grew quiet, you knew he was up to or into something. I know that she went through a rough time during her pregnancy. She was a very special woman. She went on to have five children, four boys and the last was a daughter. God blessed her with a beautiful family.

The winter was finally giving way to spring. We were busy at school with term tests, the spring play, and Glee club. It was fun to watch the boys start practicing for baseball. I enjoyed the class field trips we took, and I was getting to be a good swimmer. I had a lot going on! I enjoyed Glee Club the most though. Between spring activities and schoolwork, I kept busy. It was getting nice enough to hang the wash out on the clotheslines to dry. I love the smell of the sheets after drying them outside in the open air. They smelled so fresh and clean. It brought back memories of when Momma hung her wash out on the clothesline. It is very rare to see that nowadays.

Easter was just around the corner. It was time for not only a renewing of life in nature but also of our spirit and searching our hearts and our walk with our Lord. *"But of Him, you are in Christ Jesus, who became for us wisdom from God—and righteousness and sanctification and redemption—* [31] *that, as it is written, "He who glories, let him glory in the* Lord.*"* I Corinthians 1:30 (NKJV). Over the years and through the many hard times, my Lord had worked behind the scenes continually in my life, even when I did not even realize it. That is how awesome He is.

It was near the end of this school year, and I was looking forward to spending a little time with Mary Jane. Then, just a week before school was out; my Aunt told me that my Grandparents were taking me to live with them. I understood with a new baby coming they needed the room. I truly was not upset about this move – I was excited, glad, and anxious. I was looking forward to living on the farm with my Grandparents. I loved them dearly, and I knew they loved me. I was, however, somewhat fearful to not have indoor/modern facilities. Like running water in the house – and an indoor toilet. In prior visits as a young girl, those amenities did not really seem to matter as we were only there for a few days at a time. Now – I was a teenage girl, and I knew it would be somewhat of an adjustment, but one I was so willing to make I felt like I was going home.

That final week I spent washing up all my laundry and packing. I did not have that many clothes, so it did not take long to gather my things. The last day of school was fun, yet sad at the same time. I had made a few friends, and it was sad to leave them. While I was packing, I came across my shoe skates that Momma got me; I wore them only once or twice. A deep sadness came over me, taking me back to that last Christmas with Momma and Mary Jane. I remembered how Dad was quiet, not participating very much in our Christmas activities. The thought came to my mind that he may have already planned out everything he was going to do. In my mind, I could hear the sound of that gun bumping up against that closet door, making that thud and me not realizing at the time what it was. The tears began to roll down my cheeks as guilt gripped my heart thinking why did I not know what was in the pocket. I could have grabbed it and ran and thrown it away. I have never told anyone about that. Its memories like these that were so hard to deal with then Momma's words came to mind - look forward, not back. Better days are ahead.

CHAPTER 9
Back to Missouri

Everything was packed and ready to go the next day. We arose early, and Aunt Tess fixed a nice breakfast. As we finished our morning meal and washed up the dishes, my uncle loaded the car. Traveling with a little guy meant extra baby supplies needed to come along too. Even though he was two, his wardrobe was twice that of ours. After a couple of hours into the drive, he fell asleep, and all was quiet. I had brought a book to read, reading always helped to pass away the time. As hard as I tried, I couldn't keep my mind on what I was reading. I was very excited about living with my Grandparents, and I hoped this was my last move. Would I get to stay or would certain events force another move? As we finally pulled into the driveway, Grandma and Grandpa came out to greet us with big smiles on their sweet faces. I cannot explain it, but peace came over me. I was home. It was Saturday, and Grandma was baking for Sunday dinner. The kitchen smelled so good. Grandpa, in his bib overalls and Grandma in her long dress, cotton stockings, and bibbed apron, with her hair in its usual bun - gave each of us a hug. It brought joy to my heart, knowing this was not a visit I was where I belonged.

I helped my uncle unload the car; taking my things up the narrow stairway to the 2nd-floor rooms. Grandma had my room all ready for me. My heart leaped with joy when I saw that big old feather bed with the big goose down feather pillows. Memories came flooding back of the summers spent sleeping in this bedroom. After unpacking and putting my clothes away, I went downstairs, wanting to help Grandma in any way I could. My Aunt was getting little one's supper ready, and Grandma was nearly done with her baking, so my help was not needed. I headed for the barnyard wanting to see all the baby chicks, kittens, along with the rest of the new farm babies. I did not stay too long as I knew that I was needed to help watch little one while Aunt Tess helped Grandma with the evening meal. They ate fairly early in the evening so they could do the milking and other farm chores. The little guy was through eating, and I took him outside to play. He loved to chase the kittens; they would run around then scamper under the porch with him trying to get under the porch after them, squealing with laughter. Then he would turn his attention to the chickens and rooster running to the fence as fast as his little legs could carry him. It was fun to watch his delight in seeing live animals up close.

It was time to go in for supper and wash up. As before we used a bit of hot water from the teakettle and poured it in a washbasin on the kitchen table to wash with. A dipper of cold water from the water bucket to rinse. Things were going to be different that was for sure, but by this time, I was getting used to change. I knew in my heart that this change was going to be for good. There would be rough spots, but most certainly not any rougher than what I had already been through. As I said before, God was working behind the scenes. I know that God puts us in places and with people that will teach us, even help to turn us around to right thinking and a right attitude. It may be painful at times, but well worth it. Take it from a person who has been there.

As we said the blessing, Grandpa took the first helping, and then passed it to Grandma who was sitting to his right. Then around to the next person. There was a joy and a peace that seemed to surround the table; I can not describe it any better. After supper was over and chores were done, Grandpa and my Uncle went into the front room and started talking about scripture in the Bible. My grandfather loved the word of God, and he shared it with any who would listen. I watched the baby while my Aunt helped Grandma with the dishes. I could tell she seemed very tired from the long trip, so Grandma and I told her to go and rest for a little while. Grandma and I finished the dishes and went outside to feed the chickens and water her flowers she had many different kinds. She loved her flowers so much that she did not mind carrying buckets of water to them daily. I enjoyed getting the water for her. There were double moss roses of many colors, cocks-comb, regular roses, petunias, four o'clock and larkspur. To see and smell those flowers was simply wonderful - and to know the joy it gave her. It was clear where Momma got her love for fresh flowers on the table. My Uncle put on some old clothes and went out to help Grandpa with the evening milking chores. I tagged along to watch, not knowing I would eventually become a pro at milking the cows by hand myself. Grandpa sold the cream and kept the milk. Grandma would keep some of the whole milk for cooking and some of the cream to make butter. The leftover milk was left to sour and Grandpa mixed pellets with it for the hogs. Grandma mixed some of the chicken mash with it to feed the chickens. Grandma would save the buttermilk left over from churning the cream into butter, chill it until it was cold and add a little salt; it was so good. I still enjoy buttermilk today.

We had our evening devotions and prayer time. I loved this time of the evening. It was a time of quieting down and reflecting on the events of the day. My thoughts kept running, wondering what the days ahead would be like. Excited to be living with my Grandparents. I was not worried about not being accepted anymore. I felt their love, and there was a peace that surrounded me.

Grandpa had enrolled me in the Over Street School. I did not know at the time, but it was a rural one-room schoolhouse with one teacher for first grade through the eighth. It was about a mile and a half from our farm. As hard as I tried to think about the days ahead, sleep overtook me quickly, and before I knew it, I awoke to the rooster crowing and the smells of cooking coming up through the register in the floor. The aroma of breakfast brought back memories of summers past spent here on the farm. I tumbled out of bed getting dressed and bounded down the stairs. It was such a joy to see Grandma and Grandpas smiling faces along with my Aunt Tess's cheery good morning. The little guy was chattering in his little boyish voice, trying to get his daddy to take him outside.

I helped set the table and put the butter on along with fresh honey (from Grandpa's beehives) and a jar of Grandma's homemade strawberry jelly. Grandma made fresh baking powder biscuits along with ham from their smokehouse, and of course fresh eggs. A breakfast fit for a king. When your days start early in the morning, you need a good meal to keep your energy up for the tasks before you. After eating, we washed the breakfast dishes while Grandma started preparing the food for the noon meal, peeling potatoes, putting them in saltwater. Browning the chicken after rolling it in flour and seasoning it, then putting it in the big pan to be put in the oven after church. After helping Grandma get the rest of dinner ready for cooking, we all got ready for church. We all took our pan of warm water to our rooms, washed up, got dressed for church. This was the routine I needed to get used to. It was so good to go with my Grandparents to church once again. There was a joy that filled my heart. I knew it would take some time to adjust to this way of living. No hot or cold running water, every drop of water had to be carried in by a bucket, and I can tell you that is a lot of water to be carried in. However, it quickly became a habit, 2nd nature if you will; I just did without thinking about it.

Two of Grandpa's sons went to the same church as Grandpa. One uncle had nine children, all boys except one daughter who was the oldest. The other uncle had two daughters and one boy. It was good to hear Grandma's sweet soprano voice once again. I still love those old hymns they sang back then. That was a much simpler time, as there was no television (Televisions were expensive, and many could not afford it or did not want it in their homes. Grandpa did not want one) and computers were not around then. Certainly, cell phones and microwaves did not exist then either. My Uncles, Aunts, and Cousins welcomed me to Missouri. It was a warm and happy welcome, not like the last time I was here, but that was all behind me. There were new adventures ahead, and it was time for me to do some growing up. Learning about life in a new and different way, teaching me how a family should work together with godly leaders such as my Grandparents.

Momma was a wonderful mother, and that was because her parents raised her with love and godly fear. I now know how hard everyone worked to pull together as a family. Grandpa and Grandma went through very lean and hard times while their children were growing up. God brought them through all of those times, stronger than they were before. Grandpa told a story of how the banker had come out to repossess their farm one time.

After seeing how poorly dressed his ten children were, he couldn't carry the order out. Grandpa then proceeded to thank God that Grandma had just done the wash and told the kids to put on some old barn chore clothes to play in. That is how God takes care of His own. My heart drew close to my precious Grandparents. Yes, I knew I had a lot to learn, but I also knew the wisdom and love these two precious people had was a strong foundation to build a family on.

We all left for church that Sunday looking ahead to what God had for each of us. As for myself, I was feeling secure and peaceful. I know my dear Aunt and Uncle were looking forward to the birth of their second child. God had blessed them for the time they shared their home with me. I will always be grateful for their love and gentleness. After church, Grandma and Grandpa had a standing invitation for the pastor and his family to join them for Sunday dinner, so there was going to be a large group at the house that day. Grandma had prepared more than enough food for all of us. After our meal, Tess and George left to go back to Iowa. Grandma and I and two of the other ladies cleaned up the kitchen. Then we all took a short nap before our evening chores and light meal, and then back to the evening church service. I had to pinch myself. I was really going to be living here. This was my home now.

At the church service that night, everyone gave me a big hug and a hearty welcome. I just knew I was accepted. I slept peacefully that night. That next morning came so fast. I awoke to the sound of Grandpa's voice calling up to me, "Oh May," echoing up the stairway, saying it is time to get up. I quickly got dressed and ran down the stairs. I was not used to such early morning hours. I was still washing the sleep out of my eyes when I was told to go outside to the well and fill the water bucket and teakettle. I was glad to do it. After breakfast, we cleaned up the kitchen and headed out to the barn to do the milking. We poured the milk into a big strainer, which went into several five-gallon cream cans. These cans were then cooled in a big water trough. During this time the milk is stirred to cool it quicker. The cans were then put onto a milk cart and taken up to the smokehouse where the milk was sifted through a separator. The separator would "separate" the cream from the milk. The cream was then put into a new five-gallon cream can, and the skimmed milk was put into other milk cans for later use. The entire process was manual and done by hand-operated machinery. The cream cans needed to be out to the road by seven a.m. for pick up, so our days began at four thirty a.m. When Mary Jane and I spent our two weeks in the summer here we were allowed to sleep late – we didn't have to help with the chores. Now that I was a permanent member of the household, I was going to be doing my share of the work, which was ok with me.

After milking chores, and in the cool of the mornings, Grandma and I would weed and tend to the garden. Then we would clean the house where it needed it and then begin preparations for the noon meal. Grandpa and Grandma ate an early dinner (lunch). It was their big meal of the day, and Grandma always made dessert. After the first week or so, I had learned lots of new "farming" skills. Pulling weeds in the garden for Grandma was one thing I already knew from my first stay in Missouri, which left some bad memories. There was plenty of work to be done everywhere on that farm, and it kept me busy. One of my weekly jobs was to mow the lawn with a push mower - no motor – all muscle power, very similar to the one we had at Momma's house. I was glad to do it. It also took a while to get used to packing in every drop of water. On clothes washdays, Grandma would heat water in a big copper boiler on the wood stove. Then we would pour it into the wringer washer, which Grandma kept on the closed-in front porch. It was quite a task to do laundry back then. There were two rinse tubs. She was a pro at doing the wash. She also made her own lye soap.

I never knew until then just how hard my Grandparents worked. It was early summer, and we were preparing for the first cutting of hay. Grandpa had a few fields to cut which was manual labor - done with equipment pulled by horses. They would make passes mowing and raking, then after the hay dried pitch it onto the big wagons and taken to the barn. Then with a big claw-like contraption, the hay was pulled up into the hayloft. Grandpa had one of his grandson's help during the haying season. Grandma and I would prepare the noon meal. My job was to keep plenty of water in the water pail and the reservoir in the cook stove. I peeled potatoes, shucked corn, hulled peas, and did all the little jobs in getting a meal put together. One more thing I learned – to kill, scald, pluck and singe a chicken. Yep – this city girl did it!

We would need at least two and sometimes three chickens depending how many farmhands there were for the meal. Grandma showed me how to cut up a chicken. Working with her was such a joy.

There were twenty-five cows to milk twice a day. I learned how to do the milking right away. The hard part was keeping the cow from kicking the milk pail over. We would always give them their grain and hay while we milked. All the barn cats would gather along the walkway waiting to get a few squirts of milk. Grandpa always kept a radio playing music. He said it helped the cows to give more milk!

One night while we were milking, Grandma started yelling for Grandpa saying, "Oh Tommy, come quick." We both grabbed our milk pails, setting them on the walkway quickly, running to Grandma's rescue, thinking the cow had pinned her against the wall. Come to find out the cow had stepped on the toe end of her overly big tennis shoes. I can still hear Grandpa saying, "Aw shaw Emmie, I thought you were a goner the way you were yelling." It was funny, but I was relieved she was not hurt. With daily chores and going to church twice on Sunday, once on Wednesday night, and helping Grandma, the days flew by. I learned to cook right alongside Grandma. We made a good team. I loved them both dearly.

Grandpa did some trapping on his farm too; he had plenty of wooded lands to do it. He had fox hides, and wolf hides that he had tanned himself, laying on the bedroom floors upstairs as rugs. I thought they were neat. He had tanned a white wolf's hide - it was a pretty big pelt, the best one out of all of them. One afternoon Grandpa was skinning a fox. As I was watching him with interest, he spoke up and said, "After I get him skinned you can cook him for supper." Being a greenhorn to such things, I agreed to cook him. Grandma overheard our conversation. Talking back to Grandpa she said, "Now Tommy, you know better than that." The three of us laughed at the thought of such a thing. Grandpa had a wonderful sense of humor. He loved to joke around and play games inside and outdoors. I guess after raising ten children you learn a lot about keeping kids busy and have fun at the same time.

Summer quickly passed, and it was harvest time before we knew it. There was always lots of work to do during this time and our yearly canning season was well underway. That took a lot of water, which meant lots of water to carry in. Grandma canned everything we did not consume on a daily basis from the garden and fruit from the orchard was canned in preparation for winter. We made all kinds of jellies, jams, and pickles. The root cellar was packed full by the time fall came. I felt so good to help and be a part of a functioning family. I felt like I belonged here with Grandpa and Grandma. I was thinking about school starting soon and wondering what it was going to be like after going to a large school and now going to a little one-room country schoolhouse with just one teacher. It was going to be interesting. The schoolhouse was about two miles from us, and there was no public transportation to get there except for my two feet. Grandpa took me by it a couple of times. It truly was a little one-room schoolhouse with swings and a slide and a merry-go-round. I would not meet the teacher until the first day of school. I also had to escort my little cousin; she would walk with me to school. The plan was for me to walk down the hill on the backside of our barn, cross the large meadow below and then up the next hill behind us to meet my Aunt Jane. There I would pick up my cousin who was six-years-old, and she would walk with me every day. We would turn around and go back to my Grandparents house, where I started from, and go on to school from there. My little cousin was such a cutie – just like a little doll. She had beautiful auburn hair that was always in long curls. The both of us would carry our lunch pails. I did this every day during the school week. In the evenings, we were in bed no later than nine, most of the time by eight as four thirty a.m. came awfully early. There was a day's work to be done before I went to school. Helping fix breakfast, help with the milking, then separating the cream from the milk using the hand-cranked separator, which was washed and assembled for the next use. Wash up the breakfast dishes and get ready for school. School started at nine a.m., and I had to leave the house at eight a.m. By the time I met my cousin and walked back up to our house and on to school from there, we would only have a few minutes to spare.

Our teacher's name was Miss McFarland. A very pretty young woman. I liked her right away. A boy, called Jr. and I were the only eighth graders, the oldest of all the kids. All of the rest were in seventh grade or below, a totally new experience for me. I was the oldest girl in the school. Jr. and I were the upperclassmen so to speak. I am not sure how many children were attending that little school at the time, I know there were more than ten. There were two outhouses (boys and girls) and a well with a pump for water. This little school was what you would call a "Little House on the Prairie" type school. It had a potbellied stove in the front the room (to keep us warm in the winter) and a cloakroom in the back where we put our coats, hats, lunch pails, etc. I enjoyed that time of my life, even my lessons and homework seemed to go easier for me. There was not too much homework; we did most of it in the classroom. Sometimes Jr. and I were able to help the younger students with their lessons. It was these simple times and living with my Grandparents and having a place to call home again that put me back on an emotionally stable path. No one can ever take the place of Momma, but the next best thing was my Grandma. I was learning many new things each day. These lessons would shape me into the person I am today. I learned to always do my best no matter what it is I was doing. No matter how menial the task may seem to give it your very best effort. What a legacy my Grandparents left me. I will always be grateful for what they did to rebuild our family. Without these two people in my life, I would have fallen through the cracks of society. I can see how God is and always was working behind the scenes. I know I have said this before, but there are many times He has shown me how faithful He is. I still can hear my grandfather's voice calling up the stairs each morning, "Oh May" loud and clear. On one particular occasion I really did not want to get up, I laid there longer hoping the voice calling me would just go away. Before I knew it, I felt a dipper of ice-cold water trickling over in my face. I got up on time every day after that. Another lesson learned.

When Saturdays rolled around, I would babysit my uncle's children while everyone went to Kirksville for supplies. My cousins were good kids. I always planned my day with them. I would bake a cake or cookies for them, and we would play games or go for walks. On days that I would bake they would always get to lick the beaters. As there were three of them, two would get a beater each, and I would save a little in the bowl for the third one. I always made sure everything was clean before Grandma and Grandpa came home.

There were times during that summer after all the chores were done we would go visiting other family members. We would just show up, no phone calls beforehand, and we were always welcomed with open arms and often an invitation to stay for dinner. I could not get over how friendly everyone was. It was so nice not to be looked at as if I was "something" to stay away from – like I felt when I was living with my uncle and his wife. If I learned anything from that experience, it was to be careful what you say about others. A word spoken carelessly and harshly can leave a lifetime of scars on the one who was talked about. Our tongues can destroy people just as effectively as any weapon. As it says in James 3:8 *"no man can tame the tongue. It is an unruly, evil, full of deadly poison."* (NKJV). Only God can change our evil hearts and by the power of the Holy Spirit can tame our tongues when we receive Christ as our Lord and Savior.

I am so glad God heals all of our hurts with His love. He gives us peace in our hearts in place of our hurts. I have learned that when I forgive those who have hurt me it allows me to let go of those hurts, giving them to my Jesus. I could feel new life coming back to me. A new beginning, free from fear of Dad's offenses and stalking us. I still hurt very deeply over the loss of my mother. I recall her telling us there are better days ahead. I can still feel her love. If you do not forgive those who wronged you, you will lose yourself to hate and revenge and those better days ahead will never come for you. God cannot heal you until you let go of all the wrongs. Let God deal with them. You just nestle in His Love.

CHAPTER 10
Growing up on the Farm

School was just as I expected it to be – quite the adventure! My little cousin was scared at first but settled down once we got into a good routine. She was more at ease since I was with her. The first couple of months the walk to school was pleasant. We were able to get to school on time, and occasionally we could catch a ride if a neighbor was driving by at that time (which did not happen often). We were always thankful for a lift. It seemed strange to me, after going to a large junior high school with hundreds of students, to see our teacher standing at the schoolhouse door ringing her little bell to call us in. Life is constantly changing that is for sure. Even with our busy schedules, you learn to adapt to a slower pace. I learned that at an early age. Even with our workload at the farm, we all took time to play and do fun things. Sometimes Grandpa would show us a new "trick," which us kids would quickly fall for. These we not "magic" tricks – they were tricks on us. One time he told us we could lay on our backs and look through a coat sleeve and see the stars in the sky – day or night. One of us would eagerly lay on the floor as he placed the coat sleeve over our face so we could see all the way through the armhole. Upon declaring to Grandpa that stars were not visible through this coat sleeve, he would release a nice cup of water down the sleeve while laughing a merry chuckle. His favorite joke was showing new kids that were visiting stars in the cow's teat. Telling them to stand closer so they could see clearly, he then would give a healthy squeeze with the milk streaming right into their face. Boy did the cats like you after you fell for that trick! What great memories to have of my Grandparents and the many tricks I've learned and "shared" with others over the years!

One fall Saturday when I was not watching any kids Grandma stayed home from town, and we decided to finish our fall cleaning. We cleaned cupboards and dresser drawers. Grandma was cleaning the cupboards, and I was cleaning the dresser drawers, taking clothes out and the old lining so I could wipe the drawers clean and replace with clean lining. It was then that I saw the newspaper clippings about Momma's death and Dad's suicide. The incident, with graphic pictures, were plastered on the front page of the newspaper. With the newspaper clipping was Momma's sweater she had worn that horrific day, still stained with her blood. I froze. I started yelling "no – no – no," with tears covering my face and neck. Grandma came running into the room - she knew instantly what I had found. I had not seen the newspaper clippings until then. Grandma and I both cried together. She then said, "we will burn the sweater" which we did right then. The newspaper clippings were put away. I could not bring myself to read them at that time; healing had not happened yet. I could see the hurt in her eyes as well. I did not realize until then how deep her hurt was, but I could see that it was as deep as mine was. Her heart was broken; she lost a dougher in a very horrific way. No one should lose a child that way, ever. Grandma would not carry hatred of Dad for what he did. I know she leaned hard on our Lord as did Grandpa and that is what I had to learn to do. *"The Lord also will be a refuge for the oppressed a refuge in times of trouble and those who know your name will put their trust in you. For you, Lord have not forsaken those who seek you."* Psalm 9: 9-10 (NKJV).

Their strength and faith in our God gave me strength. It was so wonderful to feel their love. We finished cleaning that day both of us lost inside our thoughts. Nothing more was said about what I found that day. Although we finished our cleaning for the day, there was still a lot more to be done. The weekend came and went quickly leaving a bitter sting and stirred up memories. Picking up the pieces we move on, not letting the hard times make us "hard" people.

School was easier, and I had very few classmates to cause distractions from my lessons. At recess, we would spin the merry-go-round for the little kids or push them in the swing. Sometimes we would help the teacher place the next lesson assignments on all the desks and clean the blackboard for the afternoon. The boy in my grade would fill the water bucket and the teakettle atop the potbellied stove. It felt like I had just stepped back in time…at school…and on the farm. Living with my Grandparents was a much slower pace and lifestyle, but I believe it was what I needed to heal.

Late in the fall, the school would host a festival fundraiser. It was a time to gather as family and friends in support of the school needs. This year we would have hayrides and a boxed dinner auction. The girls would prepare a boxed lunch for two, and the proceeds from the winning bids would go to supply wood for the stove, chalk, erasers, books for the school, along with other school supplies. I was excited about the whole process of preparing the meal and putting our entry on the table. Grandma helped me prepare a meal for two. Fried chicken, chips, brownies and a couple of sodas. We filled my box, wrapped it in pretty paper and placed a bright bow on top. The boys would then bid on the box of their choice with the highest bidder getting the box. They would then find the girl who made the box and then find a nice quiet spot to enjoy the meal together, hopefully enjoying each other's company. I looked forward to the event thinking the only eighth-grade boy would bid on my box. I had told him which one was mine as there were going to be other boxes from all around that community entering this box social. To my disappointment, my Uncle outbid everyone for my box. I know he was just protecting me since there were several older boys bidding on it. I was sad but knew he was doing what he thought was best. Jr. and I did get to sit together on the hayride, chatting and enjoying each other's company. It was a fun time. That evening comes to mind at times during the fall of the year.

Grandpa and Grandma began preparing for winter. I helped to put clear heavy plastic over the first-floor windows and doors along with the screened-in porch. None of us felt comfortable to climb up the ladder to do the second floor, so those windows remained unwrapped during the winter months. There was also butchering to be done. One bull six months old and one hog around the same age. I was about to get my first lesson in this process, and I sure did not realize the work involved. I will not go into any detail, but it is something to see. After the bull and pig were butchered, Grandpa would hang the meat up for a short time to season. Then days later; he would cut it up and cook it then can it in jars. Grandpa would cure bacon and hams in the smokehouse from the pig. It would take days for this entire process to complete. I remember coming home from school one day to a large pot of something cooking on the stove. I lifted the lid to take a peek as it smelled delicious and in the pot staring back at me was the hog's head. I let out a screech asking Grandma, "Why are you cooking that pig's head? – yucky!" She started to laugh and said that she was making head cheese. I never did eat any of it, but others say it is delicious - I take their word for it. Grandma used every part of the pig except for the tail. She even cleaned and cooked the pig's feet, then pickled them. They were very good.

There were times when Grandpa would go out and shoot a rabbit or squirrel, and Grandma would cook them for breakfast the next day. After Grandpa skinned and cleaned them, she would soak them in salt water, setting them in the fridge. With all the meat canned and the hams smoked and bacon cured hanging in the smokehouse, we were finally all ready for winter. I still marvel at how their lifestyle was so much different from what I had as a city girl. They survived and even thrived on that old farm. They ate like kings and slept like babies – they truly had a wonderful life. Our first snow that year was not too bad, but it was cold enough for me to wear jeans under my skirt for school. Sometimes the wind would blow so hard that we would walk backward just to get relief from it smacking us in our face. We did not dawdle, lolly-gag, poke around, whatever you call it today – we made good time getting to school on those days. I am very thankful I do not have to get out in weather like that today.

The first winter snow apples were ready for eating. They are large red apples with a snow-white flesh inside. They do not ripen until the first frost - at least that is what Grandpa told me. After digging an arm's length hole in the ground, you would line it with straw making a manger of sorts and put the apples in there – then cover it with straw and leaves for safekeeping. One night after gathering a few apples for eating, Grandpa came into the kitchen stating someone had stolen some of the apples. He was sure it was the kids down the road from us, saying it looked like a hand had just moved the straw and leaves and whoever it was simply helped themselves to the apples. He then decided to set a small trap. That following night he came in with a sheepish smile on his face proclaiming he caught the bandit, which turned out to be a raccoon. He then put chicken wire over the hole where the apples lay and secured it with a heavy rock. Problem solved – we all got a good laugh at our bandit. As the winter season progressed, we would make sure our woodpile was well stocked for the cook stove in the kitchen and the potbellied stove in the front room. As Christmas drew near, Grandpa and I took the lumber wagon with the horses into the woods down the hill back of the barn, to pick out our Christmas tree. It was a beautiful snowy Saturday morning. The winter birds were fluttering around in a background of snow. The blue jays, cardinals, and woodpeckers, making their rat-a-tat sounds. We finally came onto the perfect little tree, just about five and a half foot tall. Back at the farmhouse, Grandpa took off the scruffy branches, putting it in a stand. We placed it in the corner of the front room. Later, after chores, other family members came over to help decorate the little tree while grandma and Aunt Jane made sorghum taffy. It took lots of pulling and pulling to get the taffy candy to a perfect texture. We had to put butter on our hands to keep the taffy from getting too gummy and sticky - it was so much fun. The candy started out a brown sugar color, and by the time the pulling and stretching finished the candy was a creamy golden color. I liked it best when it was just a little warm and soft. "Yummy."

That week we got heavy snow. It was a windy and cold treading through the snowdrifts to get to school. I had worn the green taffeta skirt Momma made for me on our last Christmas together. Even though I had jeans on under my skirt with boots, coat and wool scarf, I was freezing by the time I got to school. After arriving, I quickly shed my coat, jeans, and boots. Getting my cup off the shelf, I went up to the stove to get hot water for some hot chocolate. Suddenly my skirt burst into flames. I jumped back and screamed with fright – there was no one by the stove to help me put the flames out. As quick as the flames started up though they went out without me getting a single burn. I was so upset over my ruined skirt, the skirt Momma had made me - I was heartbroken. I had to wear my jeans the rest of that day. By the time I got home that night, Grandpa was waiting for me. As I carried what was left of my skirt in the house, he asked what happened. I told him how the skirt suddenly burst into flames as I neared the stove for hot water and how it just went out without burning me. He told me the Lord had told him to pray for me, which he did immediately. Our God to the rescue again.

Grandpa always paid me a very good allowance every week for helping with all the chores. I saved part of it for Christmas, their birthdays, and simple things for myself. On trips to town, I would look through the General Store to get some ideas for gifts for them. It was going to take some time to find very special gifts for two very special people. The past six months were a blessing, a start of a new journey in my life. Yes, there were rough spots, but that is life. I still missed Mary Jane and our Saturday afternoon movies and Sunday afternoon roller skating, but I was finally at a place where I felt I was a valued member.

My Grandpa suggested I sell my roller skates. It was a very hard thing for me do as they were the last link I had to Momma. They were brand new, and I had only worn them once, but with the nearest roller rink twenty miles away there was no chance of going enough to enjoy them and my feet were growing. I cried alone in my room just thinking about it, but I knew it was time to let go. One day at a time was all I could handle though. There was sadness in our hearts, but we looked forward to spending Christmas with family. No family from Iowa was going to make the trip south; it was personal family time for them. Grandma and I did some baking and made extra for the widow and her children down the road. There was also a family in town she would give food and support to frequently. Grandma loved baking and fixing food for others as well as her own family. As Christmas neared, I finally just bought their gifts from the General Store in Green Castle since I was not able to find a way to get to Kirksville. I do not recall what I got them but I know I took great care in picking it out. They gave me my first bible. Christmas came and went. It was festive but quiet - I think the events from the last two years still lingered in the corners of our minds. It was such a sad and tragic time, each of us dealing with our grief in our own way. Our thoughts would go back to that day, reliving the tragic death of Momma on January 5, 1952.

Grandma had made a pallet of soft blankets for her and me to lay on for our afternoon nap behind the potbellied stove. As we lay there, we talked about Momma, remembering how special she was to all of us. Grandma and I hugged each other and were thankful for the love she had left in our hearts for her. It was as if she left a part of herself with each of us. As long as we live, she is alive in us. I was missing Mary Jane, but I knew she was working and wouldn't be getting any time off. She quit school the year that she was in the eighth grade and moved in with a family to take care of their little boy, similar to nanny work. They were very good to her. I was glad for that but disappointed she left school. It just was so sad to me that we had lost our closeness. We just seemed to outgrow that childhood bond or life's circumstances changed that for us. On New Year's Day, Grandma and I finished our daily work early. She wanted to go to Green Castle to do some shopping and visiting friends. She said, "What you do on New Year's Day is what you will be doing all year long." Putting on our good clothes, we were off to town…on foot. We had just gone a short way when a neighbor heading to town gave us a ride, and within a few minutes, we were in Green Castle. Everyone greeted us warmly. In a small town, everyone knows you and most are willing to help whenever and wherever it is needed. We did some shopping and visiting, then started to head for home. Again, after going a little way, another neighbor gave us a lift home. Once home, we put our things away and started the evening meal, which was always a light meal. I was learning how to cook – and it was becoming second nature to me. Grandma did not use recipes too often, so I had to remember just how she did things. Most of her culinary skills were lessons passed down over generations. I remember the first full meal my grandmother let me plan and prepare myself. I took great care in the preparation of that meal. I made sure everything was done to perfection, or at least I thought. After saying grace, Grandpa took his favorite piece of the chicken (browned perfectly) and passed the plate to Grandma. As each of us filled our plates, Grandpa mentioned how everything looked and smelled so good. He always liked the chicken gizzard and would start there first. As he sliced into the gizzard, grit and sand came spilling out. With a shocked look on his face, he said, "Aw shaw May, you didn't clean the gizzard out!" I think I was just as shocked as he was. I quickly apologized, my face completely red. Grandma got him a clean plate saying, "Tommy, May did a great job on everything else." Grandpa smiled and winked at me, and we all started laughing. It is a lot of work in preparing a live chicken for the dinner table. From then on; I always made sure I split the gizzard open and pulled out the lining, sand, and grit. The lessons you learn by trial and error are the ones you remember the most. I look back and laugh at it now. I did not realize how precious those days with my Grandparents were and how much they taught me about life in general. Like the time I told Grandpa a lie, and he caught me in it. He grabbed a little willow switch from the tree and was going to swat me with it for telling him a lie. I thought to myself I can outrun him. He is too old to catch me. I took out running toward the back of the barn, but Grandpa knew a shortcut. He may have been older and slower – but he was much wiser. By the time I got to the back of the barn, Grandpa was there waiting for me. To my great surprise, with a stern but loving voice, he told me, "If you had told the truth I would not need to correct you." Those few switches across my legs really did not hurt me – because I felt his love and saw the hurt in his eyes. For the first time, I knew what it was to be corrected out of love and by a gentle man who was not filled with anger. I never lied to my grandfather again; I loved him too much to do so. Even though the work was hard the peace and love we shared was a healing time for the three of us.

Every Sunday, Grandpa would go and pick up some children down the street for church. We all would ride in the back of Grandpa's red pick-up. We got to know each other quite well and became good friends. I remember being invited to spend Sunday afternoons at their farm. The girls would go fishing in their pond with cane poles and worms (if we could dig any up) or wadded up bread balls. It was fun just laying back and enjoying the sounds of nature like frogs croaking, birds singing and of course a noisy woodpecker. Sometimes, we would talk about the future and what we hoped it would be like. Sometimes our dreams were like a Cinderella story. It is funny now, I do not remember getting many fish, but we did manage to snag one or two.

In this family there were seven children, all good kids and every one of them were hard workers. That family holds a special place in my heart. They also had a hard life. Our God watches over all of us even if we don't know it at the time.

Grandma and Grandpa Billington.
Late 1940s

CHAPTER 11
Keep Looking Forward

"Yet in all these things we are more than conquerors through Him who loved us. For I am persuaded that neither death nor life, nor angels, nor principalities nor powers, nor things present nor things to come, nor height, nor depth, nor any other created thing shall be able to separate us from the love of God which is in Christ Jesus our Lord." Romans 8:37-39 (NKJV).

For my ninth grade year, Grandpa sent me to a Christian school in Kirksville, which was twenty miles away. I lived in the dorm during the week and went home on the weekends. It was a life changing experience but a good change. Our breakfast was at 7 a.m., chapel at 8 a.m., and school classes started at 9 a.m. On Wednesday nights, church services at 7 p.m.

There was a lot of musical talent amongst my classmates, the music was awesome, and the singers were great. What a wonderful atmosphere it was. I do believe it was where God wanted me to be. What a change from that little one-room schoolhouse in Green Castle. I made many new friends that year. There were days that I struggled with bad dreams of finding the gun that shot Momma or dreaming that Dad was chasing me, or remembering Momma's bullet-ridden blood stained sweater I found. The guilt and stress were so heavy at times I would have to hide away in prayer. As always, I had learned just to stuff all the hurts down deep. As I look back, that did more harm than good. I became an expert at covering up all the hurts, guilt and wounds from what had happened. The wounds were still too fresh. It had only been two and a half years since Momma's death. I missed my daily prayer time with Grandpa and Grandma. I got good at putting on my happy face to family and friends. It was my way of not dealing with my emotions. Even though prayer time helped, I did not know how to let go of the hurts. I truly was a mixed-up young teenager. I am positive that all of us have deep hurts and wounds that we want to keep hidden. I believe my Grandfather was wise putting me in a Christian school. It taught me how powerful God's word is. I can see how it builds a strong foundation for when we enter into adulthood, in preparing us to lean on God's wisdom and His strength. I truly can see His working behind the scenes constantly in my life, even if I did not see it at the time. The older I get, the more I see God turning ugly things that hurt me, wounds that remain open, and a life shattered into a million pieces, into a beautiful, strong life that can be used by Him. In ways that we can never begin to imagine.

In the middle of my tenth-grade year, my grandmother had a stroke that left her unable to care for herself. I left school to return home. It was a hard blow for me; I liked school and made many friends. Grandpa enrolled me in the high school in Green City – it was the town over from Green Castle and was a bigger school system. I was able to ride the school bus this time.

It was hard to see Grandma so incapacitated. She was the one always taking care of others with a smile on her face. Grandpa was only milking one or two cows by then, and that saved us a lot of extra work and time. I know it was so hard for Grandpa with Grandma being completely bed-ridden. He rented a hospital bed and put it in the front room. I can still remember the loving care he gave Grandma. At first, she could talk and let us know what she wanted. I remember giving Grandma her baths and combing her long hair, then braiding it for her. She loved her back rubs. I would feed her breakfast. Grandpa would read out of the bible to her. Then she was ready for her nap. After her nap, I would carry Grandma into the kitchen, and she would watch me prepare lunch. She was down to skin and bones, so it was easy to carry her. She would help me dry the lunch dishes as best she could while I washed.

It was the summer after my tenth-grade year that Grandma had another stroke; this one was worse. She could no longer talk clearly, and other family members had to come by and help. When school started again, most of the family that lived close by was pitching in and caring for Grandma, keeping her in their home for a month or so, and then another family member would step in and do the same. This went on for a little over a year. I could see it taking its toll on Grandpa. He loved his Emma Jane dearly. I can remember when they would get into little spats, Grandma's black eyes would just snap as she was saying "Now, Tommy." but it would be over quickly. Grandpa would smile at her and chuckle to himself saying it is all right Emma.

That fall, Grandpa went to get wood for the winter by himself while I stayed with Grandma. I knew this would take most of the day. He left after his morning chores. It was early afternoon when the Lord told me to pray for Grandpa's safety. I immediately knelt down and started praying. By late afternoon Grandpa was back with the wagon filled with wood. As he came into the house, I saw large scratches all over his hands, face, and neck. Completely concerned I asked him what happened. He told me how his foot got tangled in the wood as he was loading the last few large tree limbs onto the wagon, knocking him off balance and throwing him over the edge of the wagon, right above the large iron wheels. As he was about to hit the wheel, he said it felt like a large hand caught him and put him upright again. I asked what time this took place and he replied early afternoon. I then told him that was the same time the Lord told me to pray for him. Our God is always with us. Truly, He will never leave us nor forsake us. God to the rescue once again.

For my senior year in high school, Grandpa let me go to a Christian bible school in Kansas City, Kansas. I was glad that I could go as some of my friends from the Kirksville Bible School were going and I knew that Grandma was getting the best of care.

This Bible school was a big place compared to the one in Kirksville. It was also a Jr. College. I had my own dorm room, which I liked. Breakfast was at 6:30 a.m., chapel at 7:15 a.m. and classes started at 8 a.m. I got a job at a large hospital in Kansas City to help with living expenses. It was just a few miles from my school, and I caught a ride to work with others who were working there as well. My shift was 3 p.m. to 11 p.m., and I worked as an aide. I had to complete a short training course before I could start work there – it was very enlightening. I passed the test and was ready for work. The cost of my shoes and uniform came out of my first paycheck. My schedule was tight. I worked two to three weekends in a row and would get Friday through Monday off. On these weekends, I would take the bus to Kirksville where Grandpa or some other member of the family would pick me up. It was always so good to be home for a couple of days. I would get to spend a little time with Grandpa and see Grandma and spend an afternoon with her. Life was so different from when I first came to the farm. I was growing up and getting ready to cross over the threshold to living an adult life. I was torn on what to do after graduation, stay here in Missouri or go back to Iowa. Mary Jane was about to get married, and she asked me to be her maid of honor. It was a very nice yet simple wedding, and her husband Bob was a great guy. They had gone together for a little while, but I do not know how long. I was happy for both of them. It was good to see Sis so happy. The two of them were on a journey of life together now. Their future looked bright. Whatever life threw at them, they had each other. I wished Momma could have been there on her wedding day; she would have been so proud. I know she would have loved Bob. As I look back at these days, I can see how far God has brought us.

I finished my senior year at the Bible School, and I headed back home to the farm. I knew I would eventually go back to Iowa to start my own journey, but I wanted to go home and be with Grandpa for a while first. I spent a couple of weeks there with Grandpa and Grandma was getting care from family members close by - I would go and spend a day with her as well before I left. My emotions were mixed; do I stay in Missouri, my home - or go back to Iowa where my sister lived. I knew deep down that my heart was leading me back to Iowa. I talked to Sissy, and she and Bob were happy to help me out until I got a job and could get my own place. I spent the next few days packing and preparing then rode into Kirksville with Grandpa and bought my bus ticket to Waterloo, IA. As we waited for the bus together, a deep sadness began to overtake me. I felt that this was the right step for me to take – but I was leaving behind Grandpa and Grandma, the two people that literally saved my life. I can still see the sadness on Grandpa's face. The initial excitement I once felt was swept away by a familiar pain that comes from separation. I would always be very grateful to my wonderful Grandparents for taking a young teenage girl into their home. Their love kept me from falling by the wayside. There was still a lot of emotions rattling around inside, guilt and doubt remained locked away in my secret place, and I would eventually have to come to terms with them. As the bus pulled in, we said our goodbyes with hugs and kisses along with a short prayer for God's guidance and protection. After loading the bags, the driver told everyone to board. I found a seat, looked out the window and waved goodbye as the bus pulled away, tears rolled down my cheeks. I promised I would come home for a visit when I got the chance. Little did I know that was the last time I would see my Grandmother. Two weeks later, she passed away. My sweet grandmother was once again singing and rejoicing, but this time with her Jesus and family that had gone on before her, including my mother.

Sis and I made the trip to Missouri to say goodbye to Grandma. Her funeral was at the Methodist church in Green Castle as the little church they attended was too small for the service. She looked so peaceful. We all knew her pain and sorrows were over. I knew she heard those precious words every Christian longs to hear, "Well done thy good and faithful servant." I cried so hard at her service and the graveside. I was also crying over the loss of my mother since I could not cry for her at the time of her death. It was hard for me to lose another person whom I dearly loved. It was then that it became clear I could not keep stuffing my hurts and grief down inside, it will eventually come out in other ways. In those days though you simply kept your troubles to yourself. After the funeral, neighbors, and friends surrounded our family with love and support. They brought so much food and were so eager to assist us in any way they could.

In a couple of days, I was to start a new job waiting tables at a restaurant a few miles from Mary and Bob's place. I never waited tables before and was apprehensive about that line of work. Sis enjoyed it though and recommended I try it - I had my doubts. Only time could prove if I would do well at that type of work. The first few days of work were not too bad, but that following weekend was a nightmare. The place was packed. I do not know how I made it through, but I did. I knew that this was definitely not my line of work - and the pay was not that great either. On my days off, I began to look for other work. I did not turn my notice in until I knew I had another good paying job. I worked there all summer and through that fall. Winter had come early and with a vengeance. It was so hard walking home. Bob would take me to work, but I had to walk home as the buses stopped running after 9 p.m. and

I did not get off until 11. I nearly froze by the time I got home. Some nights a nice cab driver, a restaurant patron, would take me home, which was truly a blessing. I would not think of walking alone that late at night now days.

By early the next spring, I had landed a good job at a nursing home on the west side of town and found a nice sleeping room for a hundred dollars a month. My sleeping room was only a few blocks from my work and was walking distance from town, so it was all working in my favor. I did not have many friends yet – I was too busy working. I sure was glad to get out of the foodservice industry; I found no joy in it. Mary Jane loved it though, and she was good at it. As for me, I enjoyed working in the hospitals or nursing homes. I loved helping those who needed special care. I worked there a few months then found a better paying job at the hospital. They had a special wing just for the elderly, with a nursing home atmosphere. Again, I found another sleeping room a little closer to the hospital. Here I had to take the bus but did not mind because I was finally on the day shift and had my evenings free.

By this time, Mary and Bob had started a family, and they were spending their nights and weekends at home. I made some friends at work and enjoyed doing things with them when I had time…and I started dating. I went out on a few "blind dates" organized by friends, but they never turned out to be good. One evening while I was out with some friends we stopped in at a small cafe to grab a bite to eat. It was around eleven thirty p.m. I really did not want to stop, but since I was not driving, I had little say. As we sat down, two nice looking men walked in and came over to our table. My girlfriends knew them both, but I had never met either of them before. I said hello as introductions were made around the table. I thought one of them was quite handsome. Suddenly he slid into the booth and sat to me; and introduced himself to me - his name was Jerry. He had just got off work and stopped in for a bite to eat. He worked across the street at the John Deere plant and employees from there would frequently come to this café after work. Jerry and I talked for a bit while the others were off in their own conversation. I told him where I worked and we tossed around a few simple topics and enjoyed small talk for a while. He seemed nice; he was polite but not much for long conversations. As we finished our meal, we started to pick up our bill, and Jerry took it – he winked at me and said, "It is on me tonight." I knew he was a little older than I was but I did enjoy his company.

One of the girls I knew dated Jerry previously; she said he was a super nice person, but they just did not click. She knew he liked me and so she gave him my phone number. He called me several times before I finally agreed to go out with him. Little did I know that six months later, this handsome fella would become my husband.

On our first date, he took me to a very nice restaurant with live music. It had such wonderful food and a great atmosphere – we had a grand time together. On our way home from dinner though, Jerry's car caught on fire, and we had to pull over and get out. The wiring under the dash was frayed and had shorted out. Luckily, a friend lived close by and came to our rescue. After we put the fire out, we had to leave the car there, and Jerry's friend took us home. One could say our first date – was a HOT date (even though it was years ago, a gal doesn't forget her first date with her husband!).

The more we spent time together, the more we liked each other, so we began to date formally. Jerry was seven years older than I, but to me, that did not matter. He had been working for John Deere for five years and was quite successful, in my mind at least.

The weekends that I worked, he went home to visit his folks in Wisconsin and on my free weekends, we would find fun things to do together. We would have the restaurant fix us a couple of sack lunches then go to the park to eat, watching people and listening to good country music and talk. We just hit it off right away. On one date, Jerry and I decided to go to the drive-in movies; Elvis Presley's "Follow That Dream" was playing. We parked the car and pulled out our snack bags from the café when Bob and Mary pulled up and parked next to us - what a surprise that was! Of course, I had intended to tell them about Jerry and bring him over to meet them, but I never had an opportunity to do so.

Jerry and I dated for three months, and then he asked me to marry him. He gave me my diamond ring on my 21st birthday, July 31, 1959. We married in September of that year and by the standards of those days, we had a very large, fancy wedding. My uncle George walked me down the aisle, as Grandpa was not in good health to make the trip. We had everything planned out, where we would live and how many kids we wanted to have. We were completely devoted to getting started on building both. I had come a very long way from the emotionally torn, introverted teenage girl who moved from house to house and school to school struggling to feel at "home." I was a wife now and ready to be a mother – I could not wait.

I would love to say every part of our relationship was rosy and smooth, but anyone who has been in a committed relationship for any length of time knows that is not reality. Jerry and I have had many, many good times and some very stormy times as well. Although life on my own after school was less traumatic – up to this point, I had not "dealt" with the anger and emotional problems that always accompanies abuse. I never told Jerry about my past before we were married. I just could not bring myself to do that, thinking the past was past and it was best left there. There were times Jerry and I would get into disagreements, and extreme anger would rise up in me, completely unwarranted in the situation, and I would lose control verbally and emotionally. I was defensive then remorseful after acting out in anger. I would cry and apologize to Jerry for getting so angry.

We were committed to attending church, and we were members of the largest church in town. We both liked the pastor and the people, and at the time it was what people did – they went to church on Sunday's - so we did too. Although I had a Christian upbringing, I had not developed a relationship with God, which was needed for me to move forward in the healing process. After going through several of these anger bouts, I knew I needed help. I made an appointment to talk to our pastor about it, which he promptly recommended I speak with the church counselor.

I felt at ease with her right away, she was kind, gentle, and a strong godly woman. I knew this was the right person and the right time to unpack my past. After a few brief conversations and much prayer, I opened up - about everything. Up to this point, I had not spoken about this to anyone – no one at all. It was the hardest thing to do, to live through all of the past again. To talk about what happened in detail and how I felt - the guilt I stuffed down inside and the anger and defensiveness I carried around still. I let it all out, crying, questioning, sharing…letting go.

It took several deep discussions with this counselor before we made any progress. I came away from each session feeling tired and drained – but safe…good. She helped me see that holding on to the anger made me unable to "give" of myself to anyone – including Jerry. I thought I had forgiven my father when Grandpa and Grandma prayed with me as a young girl. Why was I still experiencing defensiveness and anger? I thought that with that forgiveness would come peace, and it did for a while on the surface. However, there remained one person to forgive, one I had not yet - and that was myself. What I had not let go of – was my guilt. I had not forgiven myself. I know I did nothing as a child that required "forgiveness," but I carried around guilt about what I could have said or what I could have done to prevent Daddy from killing Momma. Which, to an adult, there was absolutely nothing I could have done to prevent it. To an abused child, however, I pondered multiple things year after year that I should have done. Therein was the problem.

I do not remember her name, but I am so thankful for her. We prayed together over my anger and all the guilt I had stuffed down inside. Suddenly, I felt like they everything just melted away. I let it go and let God take over, and then the healing process began. I gave it all to God, and He has put me back together, strong and whole, into a place of peace and beauty. I have shared the stories of my past with my husband, and he preciously loves me even more.

I often wish I could talk to Mom about some of these memories; it would clear up many questions that remain. Though I know, some questions are best left unanswered, and after all these years there are other things I devote my time and attention to. I have learned to give it to the Lord.

After six years of marriage, God blessed Jerry and me with a beautiful daughter.

We celebrated our 50th anniversary with family and friends in 2009.

This is my story of how my almighty, awesome God protected His little girls. My sweet Sissy is now in heaven with Momma and all our family members that have gone on to be with the Lord. She and Bob raised four children. Her second son is also in heaven with her along with her husband, Bob.... and my sweet Jerry.

"For the Lord your God, the great and awesome God is among you," Deuteronomy 7:21b (NKJV). *"You are my hiding place and my shield; I hope in your word,"* Psalm 119:114 (NKJV).

⟡ABOUT THE AUTHOR

Writing this book was one of the hardest things I had to do, but I knew in my heart that this story should be shared. God laid this on my heart for years to write my story, and with his help, I did. I know there are others who have gone through the same thing and I can tell you God does not want us to carry such a heavy burden.

I now reside in Texas, living near our daughter and her husband. We are thankful for their labor of love. Her husband built us a beautiful home on their place. After years of living so far apart, it is wonderful to be so close to them in our golden years. The telling of my story has helped me completely heal. My Momma was right - we must always look ahead not back.

(to be placed at the publisher's discretion – preferably at the end of the book)

BROKEN AND WOUNDED

I was broken and wounded and of no use, was blind and could not see, was deaf and could not hear. My heart was broken and wounded and could not feel. I was so alone and lost. Fear had gripped every fiber of my being. Broken and wounded and in total despair, I cried out to God. At once, a light appeared in my soul so gentle and warm filling my very being with a voice filled with such love; I knew at once it was my Lord. He said to me take my yoke upon you and I will give you rest. Trust in me, and I will make you whole. I will heal your wounds and cleanse your soul. Come follow me, and I will make you become a fisher of men then you can bring others who are broken and wounded back to me.

HIS PRECIOUS HANDS

How precious and tiny are the hands of our Lord at his birth. When his mother Mary held those tiny hands in her own, she must have known the great tasks they would perform in time. The baby hands held his mother's as he learned to walk. Time quickly flew, and baby hands became a young child's hands that learned new skills every day. Maybe they played in the dirt and petted puppy dogs and kittens. They were folded in saying his very first prayer. The young hands all too quickly grew into fine strong hands that learned to be carpenter hands building things strong. Hands that were always willing to do. His blessed hands held the small children with love and tenderness as he blessed them. His hands calmed the stormy sea and fed the multitudes. They healed the sick. The blind they made to see. Loving, gentle hands washed the disciple's feet. They touched the unclean and made them whole. Made crippled legs to walk. Precious hands touched with loving care to uplift and hold broken bodies and souls so that they would become strong and whole. Such strong, loving hands knew hard work. They were strong it is true because they still hold you and me. They hold a very special mark of love that will remain throughout eternity. The ugly but beautiful scars of pain and undying love that lets us be his bride on that great and beautiful day when we will fly away to him. Fill my hands with your love and gentleness that they too will always be busy with caring for others and pointing the way to you my Jesus. Hands that will let you work through them to care for others and to hold the hurting with tender love and concern. Your precious nail scared hands are so very gentle and strong. I have not been the same since I have felt their touch on me. Thank you. Thank you my Jesus.

Printed in the United States
By Bookmasters